Financial Planning for the Utterly Confused

Financial Planning for the Utterly Confused

Joel Lerner

Fourth Edition

McGraw-Hill, Inc.

New York   San Francisco   Washington, D.C.   Auckland   Bogotá
Caracas   Lisbon   London   Madrid   Mexico City   Milan
Montreal   New Delhi   San Juan   Singapore
Sydney   Tokyo   Toronto

Library of Congress Cataloging-in-Publication Data

Lerner, Joel J.
    Financial planning for the utterly confused / Joel Lerner.—4th
ed.
      p.   cm.
    ISBN 0-07-037646-8:   —ISBN 0-07-037647-6 (pbk.):
    1. Finance, Personal—United States.   2. Investments—United
States.
    HG179.L45   1994
    332.024—dc20   94-9676
                                            CIP

3 4 5 6 7 8 9 0 DOC/DOC 9 0 9 8 7 6 5

ISBN 0-07-037646-8 (hc)
ISBN 0-07-037647-6 (pbk)

*The sponsoring editor for this book was Philip Ruppel, the editing supervisor
was Mitsy Kovacs, and the production supervisor was Pamela A. Pelton. It was
set in Palatino by McGraw-Hill's Professional Book Group composition unit.*

Printed and bound by R. R. Donnelley & Sons Company.

This book is printed on acid-free paper.

To the members of the middle class—who pay for both the tax shelters of the rich and the social programs of the poor but end up with nothing for themselves

Contents

Preface

I am a teacher, not a stockbroker, bank executive, or insurance salesperson. My specialty isn't fancy jargon, hucksterism, or statistics. Rather, it's explaining financial and economic matters to ordinary people in plain English. That's what *Financial Planning for the Utterly Confused* is all about.

The larger portion of this book (Part 1) consists of an easy-to-read, alphabetically arranged listing of the various kinds of investments—financial instruments, as they are called—which the typical investor is likely to be interested in. You won't find tips on high-flying stocks that promise to help you double your money overnight. As you already know, no one can make such promises with any certainty. What you will find here is an honest appraisal of the advantages, disadvantages, costs, and benefits of each type of financial instrument—an appraisal based on current tax laws and their effects upon you, the investor.

Part 1 will inform you of the various financial instruments that are available today, breaking each down into understandable reading.

Part 2 discusses financial planning for that inevitable time of retirement, covering topics that every individual must understand in order to make the latter years ones of joy rather than struggle.

A glossary of common financial terms is provided to serve as a handy reference tool as you read the money-managing columns in your daily newspaper or your favorite magazine. It should help you penetrate some of the verbal fog generated by brokers, bankers, salespeople, and especially government agencies that enforce the many financial policies of the Clinton administration.

My hope is that *Financial Planning for the Utterly Confused* will be a valuable tool for the millions of Americans who need help in managing their small- to medium-sized investment plans. The information in this book can be the first building block in the creation of a secure and comfortable financial future that only you can initiate. There is a saying that sums up financial planning in 10 two-letter words:

> If it is to be
> It is up to me.

Joel Lerner

Financial Planning for the Utterly Confused

PART 1

Financial Instruments from A to Z

1

Introduction to Financial Planning

Money never changes, only pockets.

The best investment you can make is in yourself. Financially you must have some knowledge about your own affairs because you cannot hand over everything to some financial adviser or broker and expect that person to do it all. Each month you no doubt receive a monthly statement of your financial position, but do you really have any idea what those figures mean? If you will take the time to learn about money matters, you will receive a rich reward—dividends in understanding that in the long run will improve your financial position.

How Do You Begin a Financial Plan?

To begin a financially secured plan, your personal and family financial goals must be identified. Goals are based on what is most important to you. Short-term goals (up to a year) are things you desire soon (household appliances), while long-term goals are items you want later on in life (a home, education for your children, sufficient retirement income). Take these short- and long-term goals and put them into an order of priority, making sure you have an emergency fund as the first item. Then estimate the cost of each goal and set a target date to reach the goal. Don't forget to consider the cost of inflation (see Table 1.1 on page 8), because it most certainly will affect your long-term goals.

You are all aware of the changing life cycle. Your goals must be updated as your needs and circumstances change. In your early years, short-term goals may include adequate insurance, establishing good credit, and just getting under way. During your middle years, the goals shift from immediate personal spending to education for children and planning for retirement. In your latter years, travel may become a primary goal. Although every financial plan will be different, each should meet certain criteria:

1. An emergency fund equal to 3 months of net income (after taxes)

2. Specific amounts for investments set aside on a regular basis

3. Adequate insurance

Also, when planning for your future, consider age as a vital factor.

How Does Age Enter into Financial Planning?

Here are some guidelines to use depending on your present age:

Age 20 to 40:   When you are young, growth should be your primary goal; a relatively high degree of risk is tolerable. Suggestion: Invest in a diversified portfolio of common stocks or in a mutual fund managed for growth of assets, not income. Speculation (real estate, coins, metals, etc.) is acceptable.

Age 40 to 50:   Stocks are still an attractive choice, but now you need a more balanced approach. Begin to invest in fixed-rate instruments (bonds) and look into ones that are tax-free (municipals).

Age 50 to 60: At this point, growth is less important, risk less acceptable. Move most of your investments out of stocks and into bonds, in order to minimize risk and increase your current flow of income.

Age 60 and over: By now, the vast majority of your funds should be in income-producing investments to provide safety and maximum current interest.

There is a rule of thumb that may be appropriate here. It is based on the concept that the percentage of your portfolio in bonds should approximate your age, the balance going into equities. For example at age 40, you would keep 40 percent in bonds and a 60 percent stock (and/or other) position. At age 60, the reverse would be appropriate: 60 percent bonds and 40 percent equities. Of course, this is a very general idea.

When you plan investments for your age bracket, consider the following:

1. *Security of principal:* This refers to the preservation of your original capital. Treasury bills are guaranteed by the government while stocks fluctuate greatly.

2. *Return:* This means the money you earn on your investment (interest, dividends, profit).

3. *Liquidity:* This deals with the ease of converting your investment into cash.

4. *Convenience:* This refers to the time and energy you are willing to expend on your investment.

5. *Tax status:* Depending on your tax bracket, each investment will bear heavily on your personal situation. Municipal bonds are tax-free while CDs are fully taxable.

6. *Your personal circumstances:* Included under this category would be your age, your income, your health, your individual circumstances, and your ability to tolerate risk.

The chart on the next page depicts the average remaining years of life of a senior citizen beginning at age 65.

Age	Male	Female	AGE	Male	Female
65	14.2	18.4	78	7.6	9.8
66	13.6	17.7	79	7.2	9.2
67	13.0	17.0	80	6.8	8.7
68	12.5	16.3	81	6.4	8.2
69	11.9	15.5	82	6.1	7.7
70	11.4	14.8	83	5.8	7.2
71	10.8	14.2	84	5.4	6.8
72	10.3	13.5	85	5.1	6.4
73	9.8	12.8	86	4.9	6.0
74	9.4	12.2	87	4.6	5.6
75	8.9	11.6	88	4.3	5.3
76	8.5	11.0	89	4.1	5.0
77	8.0	10.4	90	3.9	4.7

How Should You Deal with Financial Risk in Planning for the Future?

As you'll learn, the single most important factor in deciding on the best investments for you is the level of risk you can afford to take. Thus, the first step in formulating your investment plan is a careful self-examination. How much money do you have to invest? How great will your financial needs be for the foreseeable future? How much of your capital can you realistically afford to risk losing? And how great a degree of risk can you and your family handle psychologically? Each of these factors will have a bearing on the degree of risk you can tolerate in your investment decisions. The sudden invasion of Kuwait and the Persian Gulf War, which followed, brought about numerous changes in investment philosophies and risk and safety concepts. The upheaval in Russia is another example of the unpredictability of an unstable world.

The trade-off is simple: to get larger rewards you have to

take greater risks. Every investor must find a comfort-zone balance of security and risk. You can achieve a balance by investing in a pyramid fashion: Begin with conservative (safe) investments at the foundation (Treasury obligations, insured money markets, CDs) and then gradually build up, accepting a bit more risk at each step. At the very top, you may have high-risk investments (coins, gold, real estate), but because of the pyramid, the investment will be small compared with the rest of your holdings. Also, to minimize loss, you should have at least two different types of investments that perform differently during a specific period of time. For example, when interest rates are low, stocks usually gain while money markets do poorly. Diversify! A series of guidelines for handling risk follows:

1. Don't invest in any instrument in which you can lose more than you can potentially gain. This factor is sometimes referred to as *risk-reward balance.*

2. Diversify your holdings. Spread your investment dollars among a variety of instruments, thereby minimizing the risk potential.

3. When investments fail to perform up to your expectations (the period to hold them is based upon your objectives), sell them. "Cutting your losses" is the only sure way to prevent minor setbacks from turning into financial nightmares. A rule of thumb is to sell when the value declines by 10 percent of your original cost.

4. Don't discount risk altogether. The rewards may justify "taking a chance." Remember the turtle. It makes progress only when it sticks its neck out.

How Can You Overcome Obstacles to Your Financial Plan?

Regardless of how well you plan financially, certain obstacles will always arise. Four factors that could have a major impact on your investment objectives are as follows:

Table 1.1. EFFECT OF INFLATION RATE ON COST OF LIVING IN FUTURE YEARS

Years to retire- ment	Inflation Rate							
	3%	4%	5%	6%	7%	8%	9%	10%
1	1.030	1.040	1.050	1.060	1.070	1.080	1.090	1.100
2	1.061	1.082	1.103	1.124	1.145	1.166	1.188	1.210
3	1.093	1.125	1.158	1.191	1.225	1.260	1.285	1.331
4	1.126	1.170	1.216	1.262	1.311	1.360	1.412	1.464
5	1.159	1.217	1.276	1.338	1.403	1.469	1.539	1.611
6	1.194	1.265	1.340	1.419	1.501	1.587	1.677	1.772
7	1.230	1.316	1.407	1.504	1.606	1.714	1.828	1.949
8	1.267	1.369	1.477	1.594	1.718	1.851	1.993	2.144
9	1.305	1.423	1.551	1.689	1.838	1.999	2.172	2.358
10	1.344	1.480	1.629	1.791	1.967	2.159	2.367	2.594
11	1.384	1.539	1.710	1.898	2.105	2.332	2.580	2.853
12	1.426	1.601	1.796	2.012	2.252	2.518	2.813	3.138
13	1.469	1.665	1.886	2.133	2.410	2.720	3.066	3.452
14	1.513	1.732	1.980	2.261	2.579	3.937	3.342	3.797
15	1.558	1.801	2.079	2.397	2.759	3.172	3.642	4.177
16	1.605	1.873	2.183	2.540	2.952	3.426	3.970	4.595
17	1.653	1.948	2.292	2.693	3.159	3.700	4.328	5.054
18	1.702	2.026	2.407	2.854	3.380	3.996	4.717	5.560
19	1.754	2.107	2.527	3.026	3.617	4.316	5.142	6.116
20	1.806	2.191	2.653	3.207	3.870	4.661	5.604	6.727
25	2.094	2.666	3.386	4.292	5.427	6.848	8.623	10.835
30	2.427	3.243	4.322	5.743	7.612	10.063	13.268	17.449

1. *Inflation:* It is obvious that if you are to plan financially for your future, you must receive a return that is high enough to outpace any long-term effects of inflation. If, for example, you kept retirement money in a savings account paying 3.5 percent per year and over the same period of time the inflation rate averaged 5 percent per year, your investment would have less purchasing power at retirement than it did when it was started. Table 1.1 is designed to illustrate the effect of the inflation rate on the cost of living for future years. Look down the column to the number of years until you retire and read across to the column under the estimated inflation rate. Multiply your plan or budget by that number to adjust for future costs. For example, if you are planning to retire in 10 years and the inflation rate is 4 percent, multiply your cost of investment or budget by 1.480 in order to reflect inflated adjusted costs. Ten years from now it would cost you $59,200 to buy the same items you could have bought today for $40,000 ($40,000 × 1.480 = $59,200).

2. *Interest rate risk:* A change in interest rates will cause the price of fixed-rate instruments (bonds) to move in the opposite direction of interest rates. If interest rates go down, as they have thus far in the 1990s, the value of bonds goes up, and, conversely, if interest rates go up, the value of the bonds goes down. You have interest rate risk with all types of bonds. The longer the maturity of the bond, the greater the interest rate risk, so if you are concerned about this risk, stay short-term.

3. *Taxation:* Determining to what extent any tax-advantaged investment would help you is a serious consideration. You must therefore take into account your tax bracket (presently up to a maximum whopping 39.6 percent), present income, future income, and investment holdings before you do financial planning.

4. *Procrastination:* This is an obstacle that depends solely on you. Don't imitate the person who says, "Someday I'm going to stop procrastinating." Regardless

of how well a financial plan is structured, if you don't follow it through, it will be doomed before it begins. Therefore, discipline yourself by continuing regular investing. Remember, it wasn't raining when Noah built his ark. Don't wait.

Now that your goals have been defined and the areas of risks and rewards examined, the next step is getting all the "paper" together.

What Financial Records Should You Keep?

Start by developing a "road map" so that you or your heirs (in case of disability or death) will know where documents are. Records that should be kept available are:

1. Professional numbers: Telephone numbers of your lawyer, doctor, accountant, insurance company, business associates, and financial adviser or broker.

2. Account numbers: Brokerage, bank, credit cards, insurance policies (and beneficiaries), and safe deposit box (keys and authorized deputies).

3. All business records (tax returns, company books, payroll data, etc).

4. An updated will and trust agreements, if any.

5. Retirement benefits: Social security, Keogh plans, simplified employee pensions plans (SEPs), 401(k)s, and the like.

6. Burial arrangements: cemetery plot, deeds.

7. Any outstanding liabilities.

The next area of financial planning is an understanding of the various forms of ownership.

How Can Assets Be Owned?

In order for you to plan financially, you must understand the concept of ownership. Joint ownership is the most common method by which married couples take title to their house and other assets. It may also be used by others who wish to share the control of some property. Let's examine the three basic types of joint ownership, each of which has certain special legal and financial characteristics you should know about.

1. *Joint tenancy:*   With this type of ownership, both owners have a complete and undivided interest in the property. Neither owner can sell or transfer his or her interest in the property without the consent of the other owner. When one owner dies, the property immediately passes to the surviving owner without having to go to probate (the acceptance of the will of the deceased by an appropriate court). For joint tenancy to be in effect, the names of both owners must appear on the deed or other ownership document.

Both married couples and single people use joint tenancy as a method of guaranteeing ease of transfer of property upon the death of one of the owners. However, it can't be considered a substitute for a will. As an illustration, joint tenancy may not automatically produce the desired result after death. For example, suppose you and your sister buy a summer home together, taking title as joint tenants. You die first, and your sister dies shortly thereafter. Upon your death, your share in the summer home reverts immediately to your sister. Therefore, when she dies, the home goes entirely to her heirs; your own heirs will receive no share in it. This may or may not be what you intended.

2. *Tenancy in common:*   With this type of ownership, each owner has title to half the property. If one owner dies, his or her share does not automatically pass to the survivor. Instead, it is disposed of in accordance with the will of the deceased. This method is used by friends or relatives who

wish to form a joint ownership and share in its benefits while they are alive but want to retain the right to decide individually what happens to their share of the property when they die.

3. *Community property:*   In certain states, husband and wife share equally in any property either one accumulates while they are living together. This is so regardless of whose name appears on the deed or ownership papers. Such jointly owned property is called *community property,* and the states where this is a matter of law are called *community-property* states (Arizona, California, Idaho, Louisiana, Nevada, New Mexico, Texas, Washington, and Wisconsin).

There are exceptions under the law to community property: (1) property obtained by either spouse prior to the marriage; (2) property acquired after marriage by gift or inheritance; and (3) property acquired in non-community-property states. Note that the fact that you have moved from a community-property state to a non-community-property state does not automatically exempt you and your spouse from the community-property law. You are still subject to the law for property you obtained while married and a resident of the community property state.

How Does Financial Planning Differ for Women?

Here's a statistic that may surprise you: Out of all females over the age of 21, approximately 85 percent will die as single women. How is this possible? Out of every 100 women, 6 never marry; of the remaining 94, 33 have marriages that end in divorce and 46 outlive their husbands. The implication is simple: The chances are excellent that at some time in a woman's life, she will be alone and forced to manage her own finances. If you're presently single, you already understand this. If you're married, please read on.

If you are a married woman, it is essential that you consider yourself financially separate from your husband. This is so even though he may supply most of your family's income and handle many or most of the financial decision. You should make a financial plan of your own and provide for the likelihood that eventually you'll be managing your money independently.

A good place to start is by opening personal checking and savings accounts and obtaining one or more credit cards in your name only. Why is this necessary? Because a woman whose assets are entirely tied up in joint accounts with her husband, and whose credit cards are all in her husband's name, may face severe financial problems in the future. If you become divorced or widowed, your credit history will be based entirely on your husband's finances, not your own. You may learn, to your dismay, that you lack the financial standing to qualify for your own line of credit. When financial need strikes, this can be a devastating handicap.

Furthermore, any money held in a joint account with your husband may be frozen by the bank or financial institution upon his death, leaving you with no access to funds until after your husband's estate is settled. And in the event of divorce, you may find that all jointly held funds are divided equally, even though you may have contributed more to some accounts.

Next, you should begin to develop an independent retirement plan, one not based on assumptions about your husband's contributions. This may be an uphill struggle. The U.S. retirement system depends largely on social security and private pension plans, both of which are directly tied to the number of years an individual has spent in the work force. However, the career patterns of women differ greatly from those of men, largely because of the time most women devote to raising their children but also because of other factors, such as the willingness of most women to relocate—and sacrifice their own seniority as employees—when their husbands' careers demand it. As a result of these "liabilities," working women often fail to remain on the job long enough to qualify for their own pension plan. In fact, less than half of women over the age of 62 ever receive a significant share of their own pensions.

The point, then, is that married women, whether working outside the home or not, must plan for retirement independently of their husbands. You should develop your own savings and investment plan with a definite goal to be attained by retirement age. You should open your own individual retirement account, invested in financial instruments appropriate for your age and income. And you should become as fully informed about your family's finances as your husband.

Every woman should have her own will and keep it up to date. It could even be argued that a wife's will is more essential than her husband's since, in most cases, she will outlive him and thus be responsible for not one but two estates—his and hers. This is so even when a wife has few assets of her own. Consider this scenario: A husband dies, leaving all his property to his wife. Shortly afterward, she dies *intestate,* that is, without a will. All the family's assets would be disposed of according to the laws of intestacy applicable in her state. The results may or may not be in accordance with her wishes.

Also, consider what happens in the event of the death of or separation from the husband. What can you do financially to protect what you own should you decide to remarry? Here are some possibilities.

1. A prenuptial agreement can help you by allowing you to keep any assets out of the hands of your new spouse if something should happen to the new marriage (death, divorce, etc.). Newly married couples may feel that this written agreement shows a lack of trust, but in truth it actually helps keep family harmony. I have seen adult children's concerns (the new husband may get all their mother's money) put aside by the use of the prenuptial agreement. To play it safe, hire different lawyers to represent each party in drafting this agreement.

2. Consider the consequences of remarrying and its effect on social security benefits. If you are a widow under age 60 and are collecting social security benefits based upon your late husband's social security account, remarriage will stop your benefits. However, if you wait until age 60 or later, you will then be able to draw on your new mate's social security account or your late spouse's account, whichever is greater.

3. If you are over age 55, you are entitled to a one-time capital-gains exclusion (up to $125,000) on the sale of your home (see Chapter 16). Married couples can take this advantage only once even if each owns a home. Therefore, before remarrying, you should consider selling your home and your intended's home so that you will get two exclusions (a total of $250,000) instead of one.

What Points Should You Remember?

This introduction to financial planning lays the foundation for all the topics in the forthcoming pages of this book. You owe it to yourself to learn as much about personal finances as possible, so that when the time comes for financial decisions to be made, you'll be prepared. And that applies to everyone—male, female, age 21 or 71. You must understand how the many different financial instruments operate and how they will directly affect your financial future. Read (newspapers, magazines, annual reports), learn (seminars, courses), ask (brokers, financial planners), and make certain that you can apply the knowledge gained from reading the following chapters so that when opportunity does knock, you are not in the backyard looking for four-leaf clovers.

2

Annuities for Today's Living

Forever is a long time, but not as long as it was yesterday.

Under the current administration of President Clinton, many of the benefits that the middle class have experienced in the past are presently being curtailed or lost because of new tax proposals. Today, either tax-free municipal bonds (see Chapter 13) or tax-deferred annuities seem to be at the center of many investment portfolios. The insurance industry's offering of the annuity has become a serious alternative for investors who wish to look for deferred income, possible tax deduction, and safety of investment.

How Does an Annuity Work?

When you retire, you will want to be able to live comfortably for life on the income from your investments. However, because of modern medicine, many people run the risk of outliving their investment income. To avoid this problem the purchasing of an annuity could be the possible solution. An annuity may be considered the opposite of a traditional life insurance policy. When you buy insurance, you agree to pay annual premiums to an insurance company. In return, the company will pay, according to your instructions, the face value of the policy in a lump sum to your beneficiaries when you die. By contrast, when you buy an annuity, you pay the company a sum of money and, in return, receive a monthly income for as long as you live. Naturally, the longer you survive, the more money you'll receive. Therefore, you can never outlive your return regardless of how old you become. It thus can be stated that life insurance protects against financial loss as a result of dying too soon, while an annuity protects you against financial loss as a result of living too long.

Details you need to pay attention to include minimum initial investments, maximum age for starting to receive payouts, terms for switching among funds, and rules for partial withdrawals. These details can be found in each contract's prospectus.

What Are the Different Characteristics of Annuities?

There are several different types of annuities. They can be categorized according to three main characteristics:

1. *Premiums:* The cost of the annuity will depend on many factors:

- How much you will contribute to your account
- The rate of return earned by the fund
- The length of time the money is left in the fund
- The procedure for distribution of the funds to beneficiaries (note that options can raise or lower your monthly annuity return)

An annuity may be purchased either through a single lump-sum premium or through annual premium payments. If you happen to have a large sum of money to invest at one time—for example, from an inheritance or from a pension fund—you may want to purchase an annuity with a lump-sum payment. This is known as a single-premium deferred annuity (SPDA). Once you have made the initial investment, no further contribution is required. A single-premium deferred annuity (SPDA) is a basic annuity which works in the following way: You buy a contract and pay a lump sum ($2500–$500,000) up front which guarantees future payments. If you die before you begin to receive withdrawals, the policy will pay the estate the contract's face value plus interest. If you live past age 59½, you may begin your withdrawal program or you may cash in the policy and receive your principal plus all interest earned on it tax-deferred. This is similar to a nondeductible IRA, since the income earned stays tax-deferred in the annuity until it is withdrawn, yet it is better because you are not limited to a $2000 maximum deposit.

Annuity income depends on life expectancy and is thus classified as life insurance. This is important for you to understand, because the classification allows the annuity's investment earnings to be treated as tax-deferred, with no tax on its accumulation until the money is withdrawn. This is surprising, since well over 95 percent of the annuity is investment while only a very small balance is for insurance. You'll find that your assets accumulate more quickly than occurs with most other investments, because the interest you earn is not subject to income tax until you begin to withdraw it. In other words, you can save in three ways;

- Your principal earns interest.
- That interest earns interest.
- You earn interest on the money you save in current taxes.

But watch out if you withdraw before age 59½. Except in the case of death or disability, a premature withdrawal will cost you an IRS penalty of 10 percent. There is also an insurance company surrender penalty (in some cases) of 7 percent of your investment if you withdraw it during the first year; 6 percent during the second year; 5 percent during the third year and so on. From the eighth year on, no penalty is charged. Make sure you find out about surrender charges before deciding on where to invest in an annuity, and be sure to ask your agent or broker about sales charges (if there are any) before you buy. These charges could affect your total yield and future income. Most companies charge annual administrative fees which further reduce your income. These fees vary, but they average 1.5 percent of the amount invested. Find out the amount of the fee before you invest, and compare the rates charged by several companies. These fees are important in determining the annuity to be chosen because they directly affect its yield. The Securities and Exchange Commission (SEC) has issued rules that now require the annuity companies to show their charges in a standardized table located near the beginning of the information booklet (prospectus).

These charges could include:

- Front-end sales commissions
- Annual maintenance costs
- Annual mortality & expense charges
- Annual investment advisory fees
- Surrender charges

2. *Payment Return:*   An annuity may provide for either *immediate* return to the investor or *deferred* return. An *immediate* annuity is purchased at the time you want to start receiving income, and requires a single lump-sum premium. The insurance company begins sending you monthly checks right away. One caution: When you buy an immediate annuity, you forfeit all liquidity; that is, you can't change your mind and withdraw your money from the investment. A *deferred* annuity, on the other hand, is purchased prior to the time when the income is needed (deferred period). During this period, which may be very short or may last as long as 40 years, your investment earns interest tax-free. If you should decide to cancel your annuity before withdrawal time, you may have to pay a surrender charge which will vary from company to company.

3. *Return on investment:*   Annuities may be classified as either *fixed-dollar* or *variable. Fixed-dollar* annuities guarantee you a certain minimum interest rate. The actual rate you'll

receive is fixed for only a few months or years, but there is a minimum rate below which your return cannot drop. Insurance companies usually invest fixed-dollar annuity funds in highly secured investments, such as government bonds. With a fixed-dollar annuity, you'll know that your principal is secure and that you'll receive at least a specified minimum income. Some companies will offer what is known as a "bail-out" provision in their annuity contract which states that if the annuity fails to earn a specified interest rate, the holder can withdraw his or her money without penalty. Because of the low interest yields earned presently, some policies are being affected by this provision. Also, if that were the case and you could find a competing annuity with a high yield, you would be allowed to transfer the funds with no tax penalty. This procedure is known as a "1035 exchange" and would be treated in the same manner as a rollover of an individual retirement account (IRA). *Variable annuities,* on the other hand, are usually invested in more risky, but potentially more lucrative instruments. The amount of interest your money earns, and therefore the size of the payment you'll receive, will vary according to the success of the insurance company's investments. However, your principal is not untouchable. For example, a market disaster could wipe out part of your investment. There were major negative impacts on the values of annuities immediately after the October 1987 and 1989 stock market crashes and after the invasion of Kuwait. Therefore you may earn more with a variable annuity but the risk you take is greater.

Whichever type of annuity you choose, your ability to tolerate risk should be the deciding factor. Younger people may move toward the variable annuity because they may feel that there will be enough time to recoup any possible losses, whereas older people may choose fixed-rate annuities because of the guaranteed yield. Regardless of which type you choose, insurance products are still among the safest savings plans around.

What Are the Different Repayment Options Offered?

As I've explained, with an annuity, the longer you live the greater the return you can expect to earn. This means, of course, that if you die early you may never recoup the amount you originally paid for the annuity. Because of the different needs of investors, there are several repayment options from which to choose:

1. *Individual life annuity:* Here, payments (which are the highest of any option) are continued throughout your life with no further payment made after you die (even if you should die only a year or two after payments begin). This plan is designed only for a person who wants the highest amount of regular income and has no spouse or other dependents who might need financial support after the annuitant dies. If you are married, federal law requires you to obtain a notarized waiver of benefits from your spouse.

2. *Joint-survivor annuity:* This plan provides monthly payments for as long as either you or your spouse lives. In other words, at your demise, your spouse would continue receiving payments until he or she died. It is obvious that the payouts each month will be smaller than the individual life annuity because the payments extend to two lives and therefore will have to stretch over a longer period.

3. *Guaranteed-minimum annuity:* Under the terms of this annuity, there is a minimum payout period established. In the event that the annuity holder dies shortly after the payouts begin, more payments will be made to the beneficiaries for a specified period of time. For example, an investor might buy this type of policy in order to receive payments for the rest of his or her life but wants to make certain that the insurance company will make payments for, say, at least 10 years. This is known as a "10-year certain contract." If the investor dies after receiving 2 years of payouts, he or she will be assured that whoever is designated as the beneficiary will receive money for the next

8 years. For this privilege, the investor will receive a smaller payback (about 6 percent less than from the other previously mentioned options). Also, if the investor should die before distribution begins, the named beneficiaries can receive the full value of the annuity which will bypass probate and its time and cost procedures.

What Are the Risks Associated with Annuities?

As we read about the potential disaster of some insurance companies (Executive Life as an example), I am concerned that some investors will move out unjustly from their annuity contract because of the fear of a possible forfeiture. If you will do a bit of homework and learn about your company and your annuity, your fears may be for nothing.

1. *Credit rating:*   There are three companies that will rate the ability of the insurers to meet their financial obligations. Examine the chart below and if you find that your company has a quality rating lower than line 3 of this chart, it could indicate a problem.

Rating	Best Company	S&P	Moody's
1	A+	AAA	Aaa
2	Contingent A+	AA+	Aa1
3	A and Contingent A	AA	Aa2
4	A−	AA−	Aa3
5	Contingent A−	A+	AA1
6	B+	A	A2
7	Contingent B+	A−	A3
8	B	BBB+	Baa1
9	Contingent B	BBB	Baa2
10	B−	BBB−	Baa3

2. *Junk-bond holdings:*   Any company's strength can be determined by the quality of its investments. The ratio of junk bonds (bonds rated BB or lower) to total assets has an industry average of 6 to 8 percent. If your company has a ratio between 10 and 15 percent, you should be a bit concerned and if over that rate, be greatly concerned.

3. *Reserves:*   Your company must have at least 5 percent of its total assets put aside in investment reserves and surplus in order to meet any immediate financial obligation and investment losses. Between 2 and 4 percent of reserves held back is a concern, but less than 2 percent should produce some serious thoughts about how your company is run and its potential to meet its obligations when they come due. It is better to be safe today than sorry later when you are ready to retire.

4. *Dividend payments:*   Your company should pay its dividends on a continuous basis. If it does not, this may indicate that the company needs cash, and withholding dividend payments becomes an easy first choice. Therefore, if there has been either a reduced or a curtailed dividend recently, a major cash flow problem could be developing. Be forewarned!

Of course it is easy for me to explain to you what to look out for, but how do you go about securing the information I have mentioned above?

1. Your insurer will supply you with reports on its fiscal condition. The company's address and telephone number appears on your policy.

2. Find out what your coverage limits are under your state's Life Insurance Guaranty Fund. Each state has set up a fund for your protection. The limits vary state by state, with New York having one of the best coverages available.

3. Call Standard & Poor's (S&P) at 212-208-1527 for an evaluation of its rating for your specific company.

What Are the Tax Consequences of Annuities?

Annuities provide certain income tax benefits that are of special benefit to middle-class investors. You'll find that your assets accumulate more quickly than occurs with most other investments because the interest you earn is not subject to income tax until you begin to withdraw it. As stated before, you can save in three ways:

1. Your principal earns interest.

2. That interest earns interest.

3. You earn interest on the money you save in current taxes.

Annuities have certain other distinct advantages. The most important benefit lies in the fact that annuity income is guaranteed for life, no matter how long you live. It's pretty comforting to retire with an income that you know will always be there. Also, when death does occur, regardless of the payout plan you choose, the annuity is free from probate because an annuity is an insurance product having a named beneficiary with the proceeds going directly to the designated heirs, by-passing court costs, legal fees, and long delays. And on the topic of life and death, never worry about life being short, because life is too short for that.

3

Certificates of Deposit— Old Faithful

*It may not seem as exciting as trading in pork
bellies, but it always brings home the bacon.*

At one time, you needed $100,000 or more to invest in a
bank *certificate of deposit.* This restriction had been established by the Federal Reserve Board in order to protect savings banks, savings and loan institutions, and credit unions
from competition with commercial banks. The fear was that
if commercial banks could issue high-yielding certificates of
deposit in small denominations, small savers would withdraw their funds from low-yielding passbook savings
accounts in order to buy the certificates. This, in turn,
would adversely affect the savings banks, most of whose
holdings were tied up in low-yielding, long-term mortgages. In effect, the Federal Reserve sought to protect the
banks at the expense of small savers.

All this changed over 20 years ago when the first money
market mutual fund offered its shares for sale for as little as
$1000. Money market funds, which paid rates comparable to
those offered on bank certificates, quickly became a favorite
investment for small savers. The savings banks began to
lose customers. As a result, the banks themselves demanded
that the rules be changed so as to allow them to compete

with the money market funds. Thus was born the certificate of deposit (CD) for the small investor.

Today, most federal restrictions governing insured time deposits in banks have been lifted, since banks are free to compete with one another in setting terms for their own CDs. You can now buy a CD from a savings and loan institution, a savings bank, a credit union, a commercial bank, or a broker (though under a proposed Treasury bank plan, stockbrokers could be prohibited from selling them). The competition among these suppliers tended to keep rates high, and for the small saver, the revolution of the 1970s and early 1980s was certainly beneficial. Now however, the rates are very low.

How Does the Certificate of Deposit Work?

The concept of the CD is simple. It is a savings instrument issued by a financial institution which pays you interest at a guaranteed rate for a specified term. When the CD reaches maturity, you will receive your principal and all interest earned. Unlike bond interest (paid periodically) the interest from a CD usually compounds, which means you will be earning interest on your interest. The amount you invest in a CD is insured by the federal government for up to $100,000 (though proposals are being introduced to limit all bank accounts to $100,000). However, it is not wise to put the entire $100,000 in one account, since the federal insurance ceiling applies to both principal and interest. I suggest that you have no more than $85,000 to $90,000 in any single certificate, because any interest you earn on the CD could increase your balance, surpassing the maximum insured sum and thereby not being automatically protected if the bank should fail. Bear in mind the following points:

1. When a bank has several branches, the main office and all branch offices are considered one bank.

2. Individual retirement accounts (IRAs) and Keogh Plan funds held in trust, or in a custodial capacity by a bank,

are insured separately from any other deposits owned by the same investor—to a maximum of $100,000.

3. Actual title to each insured account must be in the name of the account holder designated.

4. Each co-owner of a joint account must have equal withdrawal rights and must personally sign a signature card.

5. "Your money is safe, so do not fret. Backed by government trillions in debt."

What Plans Should You Make When Purchasing a CD?

There are two primary considerations in planning for your investment in a CD:

1. *Term:*   The most popular type of CD is the 6-month certificate, but CDs are available with maturities ranging from 7 days to 10 years. During the term of your CD, the money you've invested is relatively costly to liquidate (illiquid). If an emergency arises which requires you to withdraw your money before maturity (members of the National Reserve and their families found this to be the case during the Persian Gulf War in 1991), you'll be penalized for it. This penalty is known as *EWP* (*early withdrawal penalty*) and will vary from bank to bank. Thus you'll want to consider carefully when you're likely to need the money before you invest in a CD. If a college tuition bill is due to be paid in 1 year and 3 months, you know that you'll want a certificate which matures at that time. It may pay for you to buy CDs in smaller denominations instead of purchasing one large certificate. Remember, you never know what the future holds, and at some time you may need to withdraw a portion of the funds. For example, if you were to buy a $50,000 1-year CD and 8 months later you needed $10,000, some banks would charge you a penalty on the entire $50,000, since you would have to cash in the full CD. You would

have been wiser to have purchased five $10,000 CDs, thus having to break only one of them, leaving the other four intact. And the interest rate is usually the same on five smaller certificates ($10,000 each) as it is on one larger one ($50,000).

2. *Rate of return:*   The interest paid on a CD will vary not only according to the term of the certificate but also from time to time (as interest rates fluctuate) as well as from bank to bank. Don't buy your CD at the first bank you visit; the competing bank across the street may well be offering half a point more. Shop around! In these times of low interest yields, you have no other choice. Ask about how the bank credits the interest earned to your account. The more frequently interest is credited, the better for you, since each time your account grows through an interest payment, the amount of money you have working for you grows as well.

As an example, a CD paying 4 percent for 1 year will produce interest of 4.06 percent if compounded quarterly, 4.07 percent if compounded monthly, and 4.08 percent on a daily compounding basis.

For long-term, a $10,000, 6 percent, 10-year certificate would pay at maturity the following various amounts:

- Simple interest, no compounding: The money grows only to $16,000 because interest is paid only on the original principal.

- Interest compounded quarterly: The money grows to $18,140.

- Interest compounded monthly: You end up with $18,194.

- Interest compounded daily: The original $10,000 grows to $18,220.

Thus, it pays to investigate these various bank policies. If you find a bank that compounds your interest on a daily basis, you may want to make a switch and do your investing there.

How many times have you seen two rates offered by

banks in their advertisements? Banks will sometimes reflect their compounding policies by listing a true rate of return (known as the *effective annual yield*) along with the no-compounding nominal rate (known as the *interest rate*) for a given CD. Thus a CD with an interest rate of 6.05 percent may pay an effective annual yield of 6.32 percent. Use the effective rate, if available, for comparison.

Banks may be forced to post their annual percentage yield (APY) as a single figure so as not to confuse the general public with two yield figures, as is presently done. Also, for comparison purposes, look at this scenario. An investment company proudly states that its instrument has had an average annual return of 20 percent a year for the last 10 years. Sounds great? Not necessarily. The investment increased 200 percent (20% × 10 years) over the decade, based upon simple interest. But this 20 percent earns only 11.6 percent compounded interest.

If you want to compare the simple and compound rate return and don't have a compound-interest table, try this formula.

$$A = P(1 + r)^t$$

where: A = amount of money you'll have at the end of a specific period of time
P = principal
r = rate of interest
t = time period

For example, a $1000 investment that yields 5 percent in 3 years compounded annually would produce $1160:

$$A = 1000 (1 + .05)^3$$

$$A = 1000 (1.05)^3$$

$$A = 1000 (1.05 \times 1.05 \times 1.05)$$

$$A = 1160$$

What Else Should You Know When Comparing CDs with Other Instruments?

Here are some other points to consider when shopping for the best deal on a CD:

- Ask about variable-rate CDs. These rates are usually based on the current rates on Treasury bills issued by the federal government. They may be higher or lower than the rates paid on fixed-rate CDs, depending on financial conditions. These variable rates are designed for people who believe that interest rates will rise. If the ups and downs of these variable rates concern you, stagger your maturity dates. In this way, as you receive your principal back, you will be able to reinvest it in higher-yielding CDs if rates have gone up or in another investment if rates have fallen.

- Ask whether you can increase the size of your investment after the original purchase of your CD has been made. This can be advantageous if you expect more funds to be available shortly (and if you expect interest rates to decline in the future).

- Don't forget that since 1982 brokers have also been able to offer CDs. The certificates sold by brokers are units, usually in denominations of $1000 or more, of larger certificates issued by savings institutions. Although these CDs are liquid, there may be a fee imposed for selling them before maturity. Also, brokered CDs may not carry compound interest (which would lower their effective yield), so ask questions of your broker before committing any funds. As of this writing, the continuance of broker-generated CDs is still being debated in Congress, and it is possible that brokers will not be able to sell them in the future.

   And speaking about brokers, if you would like to find out about the discipline record of your broker, you can call the National Association of Securities Dealers at 1-800-289-9999. If there is a problem, you will receive a written summary of any action that has been taken. Bear in mind that your broker will be informed of your request. In this age of uncertainty, you have the right to know not only about the conduct of your broker but about the remedies that are afforded to you. Depending on the state that you live in, your broker may be liable for different acts (misrepresentation, churning, nondisclosure, etc.) but you must be able to prove any wrongdoing. In order to do so, you must show that he or she knew about your financial background and investment goals but did not follow through with the investments sold to you. If you feel that you have a justifiable claim and wish to go to arbitration, call (212) 858-4000 and ask for an arbitration kit. You can also inquire at the SEC Office of Consumer Affairs at (202) 272-7440.

- Inquire about some hybrid types of bank CDs. For example:

  1. *Odd terms:* This type offers unusual lengths of time until maturity (7 months, 13 months, etc.), which, by the way, makes it very difficult to compare yields with those of other instruments.

  2. *No early withdrawal penalty:* Although most banks still charge an early withdrawal penalty (EWP), some are now offering a "no penalty" CD. However, these "no penalties" may pay a lower interest rate than the traditional CDs; so compare both yields to determine if the "no penalty" clause is worth the difference.

  3. *Step-ups:* This type of CD pays a rising rate of interest periodically (usually every 6 months) if interest rates rise. *Warning:* Watch out when you see advertisements about these "step-ups," because the banks usually quote only the last (and highest) rate, which does not represent all the earlier interest rates that were received by one holding on to these CDs.

- Know what questions to ask of your banker or broker before buying:

  1. I am not concerned about yield or rate, but how much money will I receive at maturity?

2. What, if any, is the early withdrawal penalty and how is it applied?
3. Do I get a better rate if I am a current bank customer?
4. Are there higher rates offered for larger deposits that will still be covered by federal insurance?

In addition, when considering buying CDs, compare them with such similar investment instruments as Treasury notes. On the one hand, a Treasury note pays interest which is free of state and local taxes, whereas earnings on a CD are fully taxable. On the other hand, the market value of a long-term Treasury note can decline drastically if interest rates rise. With a CD, a sharp increase in interest rates can be much less painful. The worst that can happen is a partial loss of interest, in the event you decide to withdraw your investment before maturity in order to take advantage of the new higher rates available. The more lucrative investment into which you shift your funds will probably more than make up for that loss. So look carefully at your alternatives before making a decision.

Although CDs are paying low yields presently, and the general investing public is "crying" about its returns, they are still being sold in huge amounts. Thus, it seems safe to say that the bank certificate—with its high degree of safety and flexibility as to maturity—will remain a popular investment choice for people. And on the topic of choice, it may be true that there are two sides to every question, but it is also true that there are two sides to a sheet of flypaper, and it makes a big difference to the fly which side it chooses.

4

Condominiums and Co-ops—A Living Investment

Rents are so high now, leases are breaking tenants.

If you live in a rented apartment, you probably realize that owning your own home would provide you with some important financial advantages. For one thing, there are substantial tax benefits associated with mortgage interest and property tax payments. For another, the equity you build up as you pay for your home will probably represent a sizable nest egg by the time you are ready to sell. And with the traditionally upward trend in real estate prices, you'll probably find that the value of your home has increased substantially during your period of ownership.

But what if you can't afford to buy your own home? What if you prefer to live in an apartment, where the building is maintained and repaired by others with a minimum of headaches for you? Or what if there are few or no affordable homes in the areas where you want to live? For any or all of these reasons, you may want to consider buying a condominium or cooperative apartment as an alternative to home ownership.

What Is a Condominium?

A *condominium,* or *condo,* is an arrangement in which you own your own dwelling unit, usually an apartment but sometimes an individual house, row house, duplex, or other unit. Therefore, you have the same control over your property as does the owner of a conventional house. However, you also own a share of the common properties used by all the owners in a particular building or complex, including the land, the lobby, the heating and electrical system, and the parking lots, as well as any community facilities such as a golf course, recreation hall, or swimming pool. In these areas you do not have full control. Control (including maintenance) of the land and amenities (pool, tennis court, etc.) lies in the hands of the owners' association, and your input into the decisions of the association is limited to the size of your shareholdings. You must pay a monthly maintenance fee to the developer of the condominium; this fee covers your share of the operating costs. In addition, you must pay your own property taxes and any mortgage you need to buy the apartment, just as most homeowners do.

Since you are the owner of your own condominium unit, the finances of condominium ownership resemble those of buying a house. You must arrange for your own financing, generally by taking out a mortgage from the bank or other financial institution. Mortgage money for condominiums is usually readily available, sometimes at interest rates slightly lower than those charged for home mortgages. The portion of your mortgage payments devoted to interest payment is deductible from your income prior to federal taxation—a substantial benefit for condominium owners. Your property tax payments, too, are deductible from your income for federal tax purposes. And since you own your condominium unit, you have the right to sell the apartment without the permission of the board, providing that the board has been allowed to exercise its right of first refusal. You also have the right, in most cases, to rent out your apartment, but the management also has the right to charge fees for this privilege. These fees can become excessive and can create a deterrent for rentals.

What Are the Advantages and Disadvantages of Condominium Ownership?

As you can see, condominium ownership can offer some important benefits. Here are some of the other advantages of owning a condo unit:

- It usually costs less to buy a condominium than to buy a private home, and, as already mentioned, condo financing is often easier to arrange.

- Condominium projects are professionally maintained, thereby alleviating much of the anxiety of owning your own home. This can be especially important for the elderly, who may want to escape chores such as painting, shoveling snow, and trimming hedges.

- Safety and security are usually tighter in a multiple dwelling such as a condo apartment complex than in an isolated private home—another important consideration for older people in particular.

- Finally, the sharing of costs among a large group of owners permits luxuries that individual homeowners usually can't afford—swimming pools, tennis courts, golf courses, and the like.

This is not to say that condo ownership is without drawbacks or pitfalls. Here are some cautionary notes to consider before making a condo purchase:

- When investigating a particular condominium project, check the quality and condition of the property carefully. Make sure the plumbing, electrical, and heating systems are in good working order. The developer should be willing to certify the condition of the structure. If the condominium is in a newly built development, don't rely on assurances that special facilities, such as a pool or golf course will "soon be available." If these amenities aren't in place and operating when you buy, you may never see them.

■ When you own a condo, all decisions concerning the common properties of the condominium project are made by a management committee and ratified by a vote of the individual owners. The weight of your vote depends on the size of your unit: the bigger your apartment, the more votes you'll have. Nonetheless, the wishes of the majority of owners will normally prevail. Can this become a problem? Yes, if decisions are made which affect living conditions at the condo in ways you don't approve—the prohibition of pets, for example.

■ The maintenance fee you pay is not permanently fixed. It may increase because of ordinary price inflation. It may also have to be boosted if the maintenance budget initially set by the developer was unrealistically low. This is something to consider carefully before buying.

■ Monthly carrying charges (building maintenance of lobbies, driveways, systems, services, etc.) can be lower than they are for co-op apartments of similar size, because there is no building mortgage to amortize. But not owning common property may not always be an advantage. If a condo building needs money for major repairs, there is no common property to borrow from. If there is no cash reserve available, each condo owner is assessed for the cost of the repair.

What Is Needed in Order to Own a Condo?

Every investment involves much paperwork, and you must be extremely careful to understand the many documents needed in condo ownership.

1. The declaration or master deed will describe the physical details of your condo ownership. The deed contains the conditions and restrictions of ownership.

2. The condo association's bylaws are also an important document for you to examine. These bylaws contain all the rules and regulations of the condo.

3. The condo management agreement (if the project is managed by a professional management company) will disclose who operates the condo, the duties of the managers, and the rates charged by the management company.

4. The title insurance commitment, or an abstract certified to date, will disclose whether the seller has clear title to the condo (free of any mortgages or liens). This document is essential when you are contemplating the purchase of a condo.

5. The purchase agreement (offer) is the most important document in your condo transactions, because once it is signed by you and accepted by the seller, it will govern every aspect of the purchase, including condition of the property, repairs to be made, construction of amenities, and simple things such as color of paint, fixtures to be included, and appliances. Verbal descriptions are not binding, so any representations must be in writing. Therefore, you should employ experienced counsel well in advance of signing any papers.

Condo ownership can be ideal for many people. But make sure you understand the terms of the arrangement before you get involved. See that the maintenance fees are spelled out, read the rules and restrictions carefully, and have the condition of the property checked out thoroughly. Above all, be sure you're dealing with an established, reputable developer. Talk to friends, call the local Better Business Bureau, and ask at your bank. If anything you hear makes you doubt the reliability of the seller, back off.

What Is a Cooperative?

As the name implies, the *cooperative,* or *co-op,* was considered to be a cooperative living arrangement with people who had a common interest (union membership as an example) and who ran the building as a corporation. A cooperative differs from a condominium in several ways. When you buy a co-op, you buy a share or a number of shares in the corporation that owns and manages the land and the buildings. These shares entitle you to occupy a particular apartment for a specified term. However, you do not own the apartment, as you would when buying a condo. As a co-op owner, you must pay a monthly maintenance fee, which includes not only your share of the cost of maintaining the building and grounds (like the condo maintenance fee) but also your share of the mortgage costs and taxes on the entire property, which are paid by the corporation as a whole. Note that you can deduct from your income, for tax purposes, the portion of your monthly maintenance fee which goes to pay for interest on the corporate mortgage and property taxes. In addition, of course, you may have to make payments on the mortgage loan you took out to purchase your shares in the co-op. If you get a co-op loan, unlike a condo loan, you will not have to pay a mortgage recording tax, because buying a co-op is not considered a real estate investment but is deemed ownership of shares in a corporation. It is also easier to get a co-op loan, because a title search is not required under co-op ownership. Instead, the co-op buyer pays a small UCC fee. UCC is the research required by the Uniform Commercial Code to validate the ownership of stock certificates.

What Other Differences Should the Investor Know Of?

There are other differences between a condo and a co-op. When decisions affecting the management of the development must be made, condo owners have voting power weighted according to the size of the units they own. A co-op owner has a single vote, per share, and the number of shares he or she has is usually determined by the size and value of the apartment owned. A condo owner may sell the unit to anyone (although the management usually has the first right of refusal). By contrast, the corporation which manages the co-op has complete control over the buying and selling of apartments. You may be required to sell your apartment only to the corporation; you will certainly have to obtain permission before you can sell it to anyone else.

Co-op boards have the right to reject applicants without giving them a reason for nonacceptance. The only method of protest is to prove that the decision was based on race, creed, color, sexual orientation, marital status, or disability. Also, some co-ops will charge their shareholders a fee (known as a flip charge, usually 2 to 4 percent of the selling price) when they sell their apartment. Co-op boards can also deny one of its shareholders permission to sublet. Although this may not sound fair, many owners do feel that they want to live in a building where people cannot come and go as they please. Finally, the co-op board will probably also have to approve any major alterations a shareholder wishes to make in an apartment. However, as with a condo, any appreciation in the value of a co-op apartment during the period of ownership will be of benefit when the time comes to sell.

The strict control over the property held by a co-op's management can be both an advantage and a disadvantage to the individual owner. On the one hand, it restricts your freedom to do as you like with the apartment. On the other hand, as a voting shareholder in the corporation, you may like the idea that the corporation can limit and control the uses to which the property is put and, to some extent, the people who move in. In fact, this feature of the co-op has been used by many wealthy people as a way of preventing those whom they consider "undesirable" from becoming their neighbors. If you're a typical middle-class person, this feature will probably not have much appeal to you.

There is one more important difference between condo and co-op ownership. When you buy shares in a co-op, you are investing in a corporation, and, in effect, becoming business partners with the other co-op owners. This means that you can be held responsible for the solvency of the enterprise. And if a co-op owner defaults on his or her maintenance payments, you and the other co-op owners will have to help make up the difference. Therefore, the reliability of those buying shares in the co-op should be an important consideration in deciding whether or not to get involved. That is the reason that lenders such as banks usually charge more for a co-op loan than for a condo loan. This extra potential liability adds to the charges. In contrast, condo ownership means responsibility for your own unit only, and a default on a condo loan cannot be passed on to other condo owners.

On balance, the condominium is probably a more favorable choice for most people than the co-op. However, if you're an apartment renter, you may find one day that the owner of your building has decided to "go co-op"—that is, to attempt to convert the building from rentals to co-ops, with the former owner as the manager of the newly formed corporation. If this happens, you will, of course, be faced with the decision of whether or not to purchase shares in the co-op. If you decide that you do wish to purchase, on the basis of your financial situation and how well you like your apartment, fine. If for some reasons you prefer not to join the co-op, you should be aware of the rights you have as a renter in a building going co-op. It is impossible to list these rights here, as they will vary from one state and city to another, because of local laws, but you can find out about them by contacting any local realtor.

As you can see, either a condominium or a co-op can be a worthwhile investment. Both provide tax advantages that renting cannot offer, and with both arrangements you own a property (either the actual dwelling unit or a share in the co-op) which has a good chance of growing in value while you use it. Therefore, if you're currently renting the home in which you live and buying a house is either impractical or just not your cup of tea, look into the local condo and co-op markets. Both are options well worth considering. And on the topic of real estate, for what I paid for my townhouse today, 100 years ago I could have bought the town.

5

Corporate Bond Market— For the Future

If a company can't pay as it goes, it may be going too fast.

Although bonds have become popular with many investors, they are still widely misunderstood. There are many kinds of bonds, and investing in them wisely can be a complex, challenging task. However, the rewards are often great, and bonds are an option well worth investigating for the middle-income investor.

How Do Corporate Bonds Work?

A *bond* is a form of debt issued by a government or a corporation. In exchange for a sum of money lent by the buyer of the bond, the issuer of the bond promises to pay a specific amount of interest at stated intervals for a specific period of time. At the end of the repayment period (that is, at maturity), the issuer repays the amount of money borrowed. You can read about the bonds issued by local, state, and federal governments elsewhere in this book (Chapters 13, 19, and 20). In this section we'll discuss the special characteristics of corporate bonds—those issued by corporations.

The holder of a corporate bond is a creditor of the corporation which issues the bond, not a part owner like a stockholder. Therefore, if the corporation's profits increase during the term of the bond, the bondholder will not benefit; the amount of interest he or she receives is fixed at the time the bond is purchased. On the other hand, the bondholder's investment is safer than that of the stockholder. Interest on bonds is paid out before dividends are distributed to stockholders. Furthermore, if the corporation goes bankrupt, the claims of bondholders take precedence over those of stockholders.

Newly issued corporate bonds are usually sold by a brokerage firm, which acts as underwriter of the issue. The underwriter receives the bonds from the issuing corporation and guarantees the corporation a specified level of sales, and then sells the bonds to the public. This is known as the *primary* bond market.

There is also a *secondary* bond market operated through brokerage firms. The secondary market deals in previously issued bonds, which, as you'll see, may have either increased or decreased in value since their initial offering.

What Are the Characteristics of Bonds?

Some bonds are issued with property (such as land, buildings, machinery, or other equipment) as collateral against the loan, just as you might offer collateral to a bank in exchange for a personal loan. These bonds are known as *secured bonds*. Bonds not secured by collateral are called *debentures*. The value of a debenture is guaranteed by the good faith of the corporation, and if issued by a strong corporation, the debenture can be a highly secure investment.

All bonds bear both a face value and a maturity date. The *face value* is the amount you will receive when the bond reaches its maturity date. The *maturity date* is when the face value of the bond must be repaid. Thus a 20-year bond issued in 1994 must be repaid in full by the year 2014.

Interest on corporate bonds is usually paid in one of two ways. *Coupon bonds,* also called *bearer bonds,* have interest coupons attached to them. You clip the coupons as they become due and present them for payment of interest. Your name usually doesn't appear on a coupon bond; it is a negotiable instrument, and anyone who clips the coupons can claim the interest due. However, this type of bond is no longer issued but it may be available in the secondary marketplace. By contrast, a *registered bond* bears its owner's name and can be transferred from one owner to another only by the endorsement of the registered owner. Interest on a registered bond is paid through the mail by check.

Corporate bonds are usually issued in denominations of $1000. After issue, however, their prices vary. A bond's *par value* is $1000, and its value at any given time is quoted as a percentage of par. Thus a bond quoted at 100 is selling at 100 percent of par, or $1000. If the price is quoted at 95, it is selling at 95 percent of par; you could buy such a bond for $950. This is known as a *discounted bond.* A *premium bond* is one which sells at a price higher than par. A bond with a quoted price of 102, for example, will cost $1020, which is 102 percent of par. When fractions occur, an eighth of a point equals $1.25. Thus, a bond at $94\frac{1}{8}$ would sell for $941.25 (.94125 × $1000).

Why does the price of a corporate bond fluctuate? This is because of the fixed rate paid by the bond. As the current market interest rate increases, the relative value of the fixed rate paid by a bond decreases and so does the price of the bond. When the current market interest rate decreases, the fixed rate paid by the bond becomes increasingly attractive, and the value of the bond goes up as a result. For example, in today's lower-interest-rate market, a 20-year $1000 bond issued a few years ago paying 9 percent would be worth more than its $1000 face today, because interest yields are lower and a similar bond, bought today, may pay only 6.5 to 7.5 percent now.

What Are the Different Types of Bonds?

There are many variations in the types of bonds issued by corporations. You should understand some of the most important ones.

A bond may be issued with a *callability* clause. A callable bond may be redeemed by the issuing corporation prior to the maturity date; that is, the corporation may, at its option, call in the bonds early and repay them at that time (though usually at a premium over the face value). The corporation is likely to exercise this option when market interest rates have fallen below those in effect at the time the bond was issued. If new market conditions call for interest rates of 7 percent, why should a corporation continue to pay 9 percent on its previously issued bonds? As you can see, callability is a drawback for investors, since it prevents them from locking in the high interest rates till maturity. For this reason, callable bonds usually pay a higher interest rate than comparable noncallable bonds.

All bonds issued since July 1983 must be registered. This means that the issuer of the bonds records the purchase and sends out the interest checks. If the bonds are registered in your name, the issuer will notify you of the call. If the bonds are registered in the street-name account held by your broker, the broker will be notified of the call and in turn will notify you. For bonds issued before July 1983 that were not registered (coupon bonds), it is the bondholder's responsibility to find out about the call.

Today some corporations have begun to offer protection for a specified period against the possibility of a bond being called. The "call protection" usually runs 5 to 10 years and guarantees the bondholders a specific interest rate for at least a minimum number of years. Always check the call provision in any bond contract you are considering.

Corporations may also issue bonds with a *convertibility* feature. These bonds may be exchanged for shares of the corporation's common stock at the option of the bondholder. This can allow you to participate in a greater-than-expected growth in the profits and value of the corporation. Convertible bonds thus combine the stability and safety of bonds with the growth opportunity of common stock. If you believe a company will move upward but you are concerned about the ups and downs over the short term, the convertible bond would be a good investment for you. If the common-stock value goes down, the convertible bond keeps its fixed yield. But when the common stock rises, you might want to sell the bond and take advantage of the gain. For example, a company with common-stock trading at $20 per share might issue a $1000 convertible bond that pays 7 percent interest and is exchangeable for 40 shares of common stock ($25 per share). The bondholder would not convert at the present time to shares because he or she would be able to buy those same 40 shares at $800 ($20 × 40 shares) in the current market. But if the shares increased in value to more than $25 per share, he or she could convert the bonds to shares, sell the shares, and make a profit. Until a decision is made to covert, the bond will pay $70 per year in interest. As usual, however, there's no free ride: You must ordinarily sacrifice about 1 percentage point in interest yield in exchange for the convertibility feature. The important feature is that there is a limited downside risk but virtually a limitless upside potential.

What Factors Should You Consider When Purchasing Bonds?

There are two principal factors to weigh in considering the purchase of a particular corporate bond: (1) the yield offered by the bond and (2) the safety of the investment. Let's consider each of these factors in some detail.

What Is Yield as Applied to Bonds?

With regard to bonds, the very term *yield* can be confusing. There are several types of yields associated with bonds.

The *coupon yield,* or *coupon rate,* is the interest rate stated on the bond itself. A $1000 bond with a coupon yield of 7 percent will pay $70 in interest each year.

The *actual yield* is the rate of return that the coupon yield actually produces when the cost of the bond is taken into account. If you purchase the bond above par, the actual yield is lower than the coupon yield; if you purchase the bond below par, the actual yield is higher. For example, a $1000 bond with a 7 percent coupon rate bought at 82 (for a cost of $820) would produce an actual yield of 8.5 percent (7 percent of $1000, = $70 ÷ $820). The same bond bought at 104 (for a cost of $1040) would actually yield only 6.7 percent ($70 ÷ $1040).

The *current yield* is the actual yield based on the closing price of the bond on the bond market for a given day. When the price of the bond declines, the current yield increases; when the price of the bond increases, the current yield declines. For example, suppose a $1000 bond with a 7 percent coupon rate closed on the trading market on Friday at $910. The current yield for the bond on Friday would be 7.7 percent ($70 ÷ $910).

Finally, *yield to maturity* (*YTM*) represents the total rate of return if the bond is held to maturity, taking into consideration the purchase price of the bond, the interest paid, and the redemption price. Any broker can refer to a standard reference book which contains yield-to-maturity figures for almost any conceivable bond. The YTM is important because current yield does not reflect any difference between the current purchase price and the value at maturity. If you purchased a bond for $850 and held it to its maturity, you would receive the bond's face of $1000—in other words, a capital appreciation of $150 in addition to the annual interest. The YTM takes all this information into consideration as part of its calculation. The rate plus prorated discount (or subtracting prorated premium) is divided by the average of the total of the face plus purchase price. For example, the YTM of a 7 percent, $1000 bond sold for $850 with 10 years to maturity would be calculated as follows:

$$\text{YTM} = \frac{\text{coupon} + \text{prorated discount}}{(\text{face value} + \text{purchase price}) \div 2}$$

$$= \frac{70 \text{ (rate)} + \$15 \text{ ($\$150 \div 10$ years)}}{\$1000 \text{ (face)} + \$850 \text{ (purchase price)} \div 2}$$

$$= \frac{\$85}{\$925}$$

$$= 9.2\%$$

Naturally, all things being equal, the higher the yield on a particular bond, the better buy that bond is likely to be. But all things are not always equal. Bonds also differ in their degree of safety. That brings us to the second dominant consideration in choosing a bond for purchase.

How Is Safety Applied to Bonds?

The degree of risk associated with the purchase of a particular bond depends on the strength of the issuing corporation. Of course, it's not easy for the average middle-income investor to analyze the performance of all the many bond-issuing corporations. For a full examination, it would be necessary to study the company's financial statements, its earnings projections, the track record of management, prospects for the industry, and many other factors.

Fortunately, you don't need to do all this research yourself. There are special advisory services which have assumed the task of analyzing and rating the safety of corporate bonds. These ratings can be obtained from reference books you can readily find at your public library or request from any brokerage house.

The two best-known rating services are Moody's and Standard & Poor's (S&P). They rate bonds according to two slightly differing scales. Starting with the highest-rated bonds, the two scales are as follows:

Moody's: Aaa, Aa, A, Baa, Ba, B, Caa, Ca, C

S & P: AAA, AA, A, BBB, BB, B, CCC, CC, C

The most risk-free bonds—those issued by large, stable corporations showing excellent future earnings projections—are rated Aaa or AAA. Bonds rated AA or A are issued by firms whose ability to pay interest and principal is quite strong, but the safety of these bonds is somewhat more vulnerable to changes in economic conditions.

As you move toward the lower end of the rating scale, yields are likely to be higher; the lower-rated firms must offer higher interest rates to induce investors to accept the greater degree of risk. The bonds on the lowest rungs of the ladder are sometimes called "junk bonds." These bonds have ratings of BB or lower and usually pay yields about 3 percentage points higher than A-rated bonds. They received their disparaging nickname in the late 1920s and early 1930s, when the Great Depression led to numerous defaults by bond issuers, and are today considered one of the major factors in the savings and loan failures and the inadequate financing of major mergers and acquisitions. The junk bonds offer neither the security of bonds nor the growth of stocks. Yet there are those who will argue that junk bonds have done well in the past. Perhaps a statement I heard about them will suffice. If you ask a drunk at 11 p.m. how he feels, the answer is "fine." The big question is, how will the drunk feel in the morning?

Most brokers will quote the standard bond ratings along with prices and yields when you inquire about possible investments. For maximum safety, you'll probably want to stick to bonds rated A and higher. However, even though a bond may have an AA rating when you purchase it, that rating is always subject to change, upward or downward. The only exception would be if you want to choose a low-rated, high yielding bond on a speculative basis. If you do, make sure that the amount you risk in this way is no greater than the amount you can afford to lose. Greed—especially for the ill-informed investor—can lead to devastating mistakes.

How Do You Learn about Bonds?

If you're interested in getting into the bond market, you should know how to read the bond quotations which appear on the business page of your daily newspaper. These are a good basic source of information about currently available bonds. Figure 5.1 provides a sample bond listing as it might appear in the newspaper. You'll find an explanation of the information each column provides below the sample listing.

Issue	Descrip- tion	Current yield	Volume	High	Low	Last	Change
ABC	6¾ 04	7.6	28	90	88½	89	+ 2

Issue: The abbreviated name of the corporation issuing the bond; in this case, ABC.

Description: A description of the bond. This bond has a coupon yield of 6¾ and matures in 2004.

Current yield: The annual interest on a $1000 bond divided by today's closing price for the bond. In this case, 6¾ percent of $1000 ($67.50) divided by $890 = 7.6 percent.

Volume: The number of $1000 bonds traded that day.

High: The highest price of the day; in this case, 90 percent of par, or $900 for a $1000 bond.

Low: The lowest price of the day; in this case, 88½ percent of par, or $885 for a $1000 bond.

Last: The day's closing price; in this case, 89 percent of par, or $890 for a $1000 bond.

Change: The difference between today's closing price and yesterday's. Since today's closing price of $890 is 2 points higher than the previous day, yesterday's closing price must have been 87, or $870.

Figure 5.1. Sample corporate bond listing.

Bonds make an excellent choice for many middle-income investors, especially those whose primary need is for income rather than growth. Older people looking toward retirement, for example, are likely to find bonds a particularly attractive investment. However, since bonds are available in so many different forms, be careful in your selections. Remember the importance of safety, and use the standard ratings as your guide. Also be sure you understand the details of the particular bond issue you are considering before you buy. The informed investor can do very well in today's corporate bond market. And on the topic of information, education is what you get when you read the fine print; experience is what you get when you don't.

6

Ginnie Mae—
The Misunderstood
Instrument

Some think that Ginnie Mae is just a little
girl and that Fannie Mae is her mother.

If I had to choose the most misunderstood financial instrument from among the many about which I write, I would pick the government-insured mortgage.

What Is a Ginnie Mae?

The Government National Mortgage Association (GNMA) was formed by Congress in 1968 as a branch of the Department of Housing and Urban Development. Its objective was to buy government-insured mortgages, similar to those guaranteed by the Federal Housing Administration (FHA) and the Veterans Administration (VA), from the banks which originally made the loans. By doing this, the GNMA provides the lending institutions with the money to offer additional mortgages.

After buying these FHA and VA mortgages, the GNMA groups them into units of a million dollars or more, known as *pools*. These pools are then sold to investment brokerage houses, with an additional guarantee against default added by the GNMA. The brokers, in turn, sell shares in these units of $25,000 or more. These shares are known as *Ginnie Mae pass-through certificates*. The name "Ginnie Mae" is a fanciful pronunciation of GNMA, and the term *pass-through certificate* comes from the fact that, when an investor buys the certificate, the homeowner's mortgage payments are passed through to the investor.

How Does the Ginnie Mae Work?

To explain how the Ginnie Mae works, let's follow one mortgage as it is created with the borrower and ultimately winds up in the hands of the investor: Mr. J takes out a FHA mortgage with the Penny National Bank. This bank combines about 50 other similar mortgages totaling approximately $1 million, and sells these mortgages to the GNMA. This gives the Penny Bank its funds back so that it can lend more money again. The GNMA can either retain this pool of mortgages or sell it to investors. A brokerage house may purchase the pool, carve it up into smaller units, and sell them to its clients, the general public. It then moves out of the picture, leaving the original lender collecting Mr. J's monthly payment and forwarding it to the investing public who just bought the Ginnie Mae. If Mr. J should not be able to meet his mortgage payments, the bank will foreclose and the government will make good that portion of the default.

As you can see, the Ginnie Mae is a way of investing in a large pool of government-guaranteed mortgages simply by purchasing a share in the pool. Since the smallest units sold are $25,000 packages, institutional investors do most of the direct trading in Ginnie Maes. However, it's possible to get involved in Ginnie Maes for as little as $1000 by buying a unit in a Ginnie Mae mutual fund or trust.

Are Ginnie Maes Safe?

Ginnie Maes are an excellent, safe investment. Because of the involvement of the GNMA, payments of both principal and interest on the mortgage loans are fully guaranteed by the federal government. This guarantee is in addition to the government guarantee which already covers FHA and VA mortgages, so the degree of risk in Ginnie Maes is as small as you're ever likely to get. However, they are not considered obligations of the United States and are therefore subject to federal, state, and any local taxes.

I know that it sounds confusing when the law reads that "states are not permitted to tax obligations of the United States" and yet everyone considers Ginnie Maes obligations of the United States. Well, yes and no. The first obligation to make payment on Ginnie Maes rests with the financial institution that issues the certificates. The U.S. government is only a guarantor in the unlikely event of default.

How Is Income Paid to the Investor?

Income from Ginnie Maes is paid on a monthly basis. If you own a Ginnie Mae, you'll receive (around the fifteenth of each month) a check representing an installment of the repayment of the mortgages in the pool into which you've bought. A part of each check represents repayment of the principal on the loan; the rest is interest. An enclosed statement will tell you what portion of the check is interest and what portion is principal—something you'll need to know, since the interest portion is taxable while the principal payments are not. During the early months of the repayment period, you'll mainly receive interest; later payments include a higher percentage of principal. This may be advantageous at times, but it might present a problem. The continual return of your principal can expose you to what is known as *reinvestment risk*. Normally, during times of falling interest rates, your payments accelerate, meaning that you will get money that will be reinvested at lower rates. Also, some people tend to forget that, with each month's payment, they receive, included in the total amount, a portion of their principal. Many times this is ignored and the total amount is spent as if it were all interest. Remember that when those checks stop coming, there is no principal left. If your broker holds your Ginnie Mae certificates, he or she can move the principal you receive into a cash management account (CMA). Thus you can reinvest in the Ginnie Mae when you have accumulated enough principal to do so.

There is a variation of this system by which you can arrange to have the principal remain intact and receive only interest payments. Younger investors may wish to consider this option, since it provides for steady payments of interest on a fixed principal, which itself is paid in full at the time when the certificate matures. Older investors—retirees, for example—will probably prefer the usual interest-plus-principal repayment plan, since they usually have a greater need for monthly income than for a large lump-sum payment at the end.

There is one major drawback to investing in Ginnie Maes—the impossibility of predicting their yield. The monthly checks you'll receive will vary in size, and the period over which the checks keep coming may vary also. The reason is that no one is certain when the mortgages will be paid in full. As you know, some people take a full 30 years to repay their mortgage loans; others sell their houses and repay the mortgages after only a year or two. Since no one can predict how long the homeowners in a particular pool will take to repay their loans, no one can predict exactly how long the payments will last or how large each monthly payment will be. Therefore, one month you might receive a large check that is an unexpected payoff of principal, but then subsequent checks might be smaller, because you will be earning the same rate on a smaller principal. If you place your money in the Federal National Mortgage Association (FNMA) or the Federal Home Loan Mortgage Corporation (FHLMC) (see Chapter 7), you will be involved in at least 1000 mortgages rather than the GNMA's 50. Therefore, the impact of early payback is greatly diminished.

To find the best "deal" from your broker, look for a seasoned pool that has a history of stability. Watch out for any pool based on mortgages with low single-digit interest rates, because with those low rates, homeowners will usually stay with the mortgage until the end (sometimes as long as 30 years). Such a pool will pay out longer than the 12-year average, which will tie up your money and produce even lower returns than you had anticipated.

When Does the Ginnie Mae Mature?

One rule of thumb brokers often cite is that Ginnie Mae mortgage pools are repaid, on the average, within 12 years. This means that if you buy a Ginnie Mae certificate, you can estimate that you'll continue to receive monthly checks for about 12 years; and those checks will be larger in the beginning than near the end, since the amount of outstanding debt will be greater at that time. Neither prediction is guaranteed. For example, your certificate may continue to pay monthly checks for 15 years or more, or it may be entirely paid out within 5 to 8 years or less. Bear in mind that the Ginnie Mae is not a financial instrument to speculate with for a short period of time. When you purchase one, you are not involved with "Ginnie" for a quick romance; you are in for a long-term relationship. The reason is that the bid/ask spread on this instrument (the difference between what is paid for the instrument and its selling price) is very costly and you could lose a great deal on a short-term basis. It would probably be more beneficial if you bought a Ginnie Mae mutual fund (see the last section of this chapter) even if it costs you about a half point in lower yields. At least you will have the confidence of knowing that you can get out at any time.

How Do Current Interest Rates Affect the Ginnie Mae?

Changes in the market interest rate on mortgages play an important role here. The interest rate you'll receive on your Ginnie Mae depends, of course, on the mortgage rate at the time the pool was established. If mortgage rates fall below that figure, it's likely that repayment of your Ginnie Mae will be accelerated. This is because the homeowners who took out the mortgages will be eager to repay their high-interest loans and refinance their homes at the new, lower rates. So, you'll get back your money sooner and be forced to reinvest it elsewhere at the new, lower prevailing interest rates. For example, the 1981 high-interest-rate Ginnie Maes (15 to 17 percent) will certainly be turned in, as any home-owner with huge debt service would refinance at the earli-est opportunity.

By contrast, if mortgage interest rates rise, the life of your Ginnie Mae is likely to be prolonged. Homeowners will be content to keep paying the relatively low rate of interest they locked in at the time they took out their mortgages, and you'll continue to receive checks for longer than the average 12-year repayment period.

As you can see, Ginnie Maes are not an ideal investment for those who must be able to predict their future monthly income with absolute certainty. If you can afford to be flexi-ble, you can afford to consider Ginnie Maes.

There is a major secondary market in Ginnie Maes made up of shares in mortgage pools established at some time in the past. Like previously issued bonds, previously issued Ginnie Maes fluctuate in value owing to market condi-tions. Depending on the age of the certificate, the number of monthly payments that have already been made, and interest rate considerations, you may be able to buy an older Ginnie Mae certificate at a considerable discount from its face value. A Ginnie Mae quoted at 90 sells for 90 percent of its face value; that is, a $25,000 certificate would cost $22,500.

If you are concerned about taking a loss when selling your Ginnie Mae, consider the following. If the certificate is sold prior to maturity and interest rates rise, your Ginnie Mae would be sold at a loss because it is a fixed-rate instru-ment. You can avoid any fluctuations by purchasing a Ginnie Mae certificate backed by an adjustable-rate mortgage (ARM) pool. Since the rate of interest is adjusted on the certificate, the Ginnie Mae should trade at close to its original price.

What Other Factors Should You Know About?

In addition to the quoted price there are two important factors to consider when you look at previously issued Ginnie Maes: the *pool factor* and the *pool speed.*

The pool factor is the percentage of the principal that remains unpaid in a particular mortgage pool. The higher the pool factor, the longer it will probably take for the loan repayments to be completed and the longer you will continue to receive checks. The pool speed is the relative speed with which repayment of loans in a particular pool is occurring. This will vary depending on economic conditions, the interest rate at the time the pool was established, and the geographic areas in which the mortgages were issued. If the pool speed is high, your Ginnie Mae checks will probably end fairly soon; if the pool speed is low, they will probably last longer.

Therefore, you can readily understand that for the following reasons, Ginnie Mae is an investment worth looking into.

1. Your money is backed by the U.S. government even if the borrowers do not meet their obligations.

2. The loans are liquid and may be resold if necessary.

3. There is a monthly cash flow that allows debt repayment to go from borrower to bank, which will then service you, the investor.

4. You can reinvest your monthly income during periods of higher interest rates.

5. The yields are attractive and higher than Treasury obligations. Also, because mortgages compound every month rather than every 6 months, as with bonds, the yield is higher than what is stated.

How Can the Small Investor Purchase a Ginnie Mae?

Many people can't afford the $25,000 minimum investment required to buy a Ginnie Mae certificate. If you're one of these people, consider buying a unit in a Ginnie Mae mutual or trust fund. These units usually sell for $1000, and can be bought and sold through brokers. Each fund has its own rules and procedures, as well as its own portfolio of mortgage holdings, which may affect the income you'll receive. When you invest in a Ginnie Mae fund, you may have to pay a sales charge of up to 3.5 percent. There may be instead, or in addition, an annual service or management fee. As with any mutual fund, shop around and ask questions before writing a check. And on the topic of questioning, to know the road ahead, ask those coming back.

7

Ginnie Mae Alternatives

The hardest lesson to learn in life is to decide which bridges to cross and which to burn.

When you investigate Ginnie Maes, you may hear references to two other forms of mortgage-backed securities: Freddie Macs and Fannie Maes. Freddie Macs are issued by the Federal Home Loan Mortgage Corporation (FHLMC) and focus on conventional loans which it purchases in quantity and then resells. A minimum of $25,000 is needed to invest in Freddie Mac *participation certificates* (PCs). The mortgages in the Freddie Mac pools are usually not government-insured loans, like the FHA and VA mortgages in which the GNMA specializes, but are privately issued, nonguaranteed mortgages. As a consequence, the FHLMC does not absolutely guarantee your investment as the GNMA does; instead, you are guaranteed "timely" payments of interest and "ultimate" repayment of principal. It's possible, then, that you might be kept waiting for some of your money when you invest in a Freddie Mac. As with most forms of investment, the slightly greater risk with a Freddie Mac is counterbalanced by a higher rate of return— usually $\frac{1}{4}$ to $\frac{1}{2}$ percent or more. Note also that the market for Freddie Macs is much smaller than that for Ginnie Maes, so it might take a while to liquidate your holdings if and when you decide to sell.

How Do Fannie Maes and Freddie Macs Work?

Fannie Maes are issued by the Federal National Mortgage Association (FNMA). The FNMA serves the secondary mortgage market by buying single and multifamily loans and then reselling them to investors by way of mortgage-backed securities. In most ways, Fannie Maes are similar to Freddie Macs, and, as with Ginnie Maes, timely payments of both interest and principal are guaranteed. Unlike Ginnie Maes, which consist of mortgages insured by the FHA or guaranteed by the VA, Fannie Maes may include either government-backed loans or privately insured conventionals. In the latter case, the FNMA (rather than the government) stands behind the debt. Do not overly concern yourself about the safety of either the FNMA or FHLMC, as both organizations are government-chartered companies, and their issues are considered to be "moral obligations" of the government. They also yield slightly higher interest rates than the GNMA.

The risk faced by an investor in Ginnie Maes, Fannie Maes, or Freddie Macs is not that the homeowners will not make their monthly payments, but just the opposite, that they might pay off their mortgages too rapidly if mortgage rates should fall. This can occur when homeowners sell, refinance, or exchange a high-interest mortgage for a lower-interest one. The trouble for the investor is that there is a sudden infusion of money because a prepayment by a homeowner will cause all interest payments on the mortgage to stop, and this repaid principal will then have to be reinvested, usually at a lower rate. This early payment problem can now be overcome to a small degree with the introduction of the *collateralized mortgage obligation* (CMO).

What Backs the CMOs?

CMOs are typically backed by federally sponsored housing agency mortgage pass-through securities of the GNMA

(Government National Mortgage Association), the FHLMC (Federal Home Loan Mortgage Corporation) or the FNMA (Federal National Mortgage Association).

CMO issuers include special-purpose subsidiaries of large investment banks, mortgage servicing companies, and U.S. government sponsored agencies. The issuer assembles a large pool of mortgage-backed securities (such as Ginnie Maes (GNMAs), Freddie Macs, and Fannie Maes) in a trust, which is the underlying collateral for the CMO. The mortgages underlying these securities carry U.S. government sponsored agency guarantees.

What Is the Basic Idea of the CMO?

The interest and principal payments from the underlying mortgage-backed securities are allocated to the CMO investors according to priorities established during the origination process. This payment schedule redistributes the mortgage-backed bonds with sequentially stated maturities call "tranches" (the French word for "slices"). These tranches are offered with short- (fast or first pay), intermediate- (medium pay), and long-term (slow pay) projected average lives. Depending on the structure of the issue, the likelihood of the real average life being very close to the projection may be quite high or subject to considerable variation.

How Do These Payments Work?

Principal repayments will go first to the class with the shortest maturity. When they are retired, the principal will then go to the bonds with the next shortest maturity, and so on, until all classes have been paid off. There could be as many as a dozen different classes of maturity. Instead of one security with a final stated maturity of 20 years, there would be many different classes of maturities (3 years, 5 years, 9 years, etc.). In other words, those holding the "fast pay" will get a portion of the mortgage interest payments and receive all the prepayments on the underlying mortgages until everyone in that group has been fully repaid (2 to 3 years). If investors want higher returns (usually ½ percent) they can choose the "slow pay" option. Under this choice the investor will receive interest for several years (10 to 20 years) but will get no principal until all the shorter-term bonds have been repaid. At that time, payments may continue.

Because CMOs do not have a single retirement date, they are an improvement over GNMAs, which begin to pay off principal the month that they are issued. Bear in mind that CMOs do not carry exact maturity dates as other types of bonds do. A newly issued CMO may have an estimated life of 3 years (1st tranche), 8 years (2d tranche) and 17 years (3d tranche) based upon statistical assumptions. However, the exact speed of prepayment will be determined on what happens in the economy to interest rates. If a CMO paying 10 percent for 8 years falls into an economy that has dropped its interest rate by 3 or 4 percentage points, mortgage holders will refinance their higher mortgages by getting new ones, thus breaking the pool of CMOs and returning money sooner to the investor. Conversely, if interest rates should rise, holders of mortgages will want to keep their mortgages for as long as possible and thus the rate of prepayments of principal would slow down and the investor might end up with a 15-year investment. Because of this uncertainty, you will receive a higher yield than you might receive on comparable securities (at least 100 basis points or 1 percent as compared with U.S. Treasury notes). Bear in mind that the longer and more uncertain the maturity period, the higher the yield.

How Do You Buy CMOs?

CMOs are issued in book-entry form and are subject to federal and state income tax on their coupon income. CMOs are quoted as a percentage of face value. A $1000 bond (not the

$25,000 minimum requirement for a GNMA) quoted at a price of 99 would cost $990. This will include a commission of $\frac{1}{2}$ percent to 3 percent depending on the length of maturity (the longer the period, the higher the commission). Don't buy a CMO priced more than a full percentage point below face value because if interest rates rise, your projected length of maturity can be much longer than expected (fewer people will refinance). In other words you will be holding a low-yielding investment for a long term. On the other hand, don't purchase a CMO priced more than a full percentage point above par because if interest rates should fall, your premium will disappear and the high rate of return will not be with you for any lengthy period of time because of high prepayments. Remember, CMOs can be sold at any time but they are meant to be held until maturity. Also, bear in mind that when comparing the CMO to U.S. Treasury obligations, after the broker's commission, if your CMO does not yield at least 1 percentage point higher than the Treasury notes, there is no reason to purchase the CMO.

How Safe Are CMOs?

CMOs are backed by the GNMA, FNMA, FHLMC, or by private insurance. Ratings are based not on the credit of the issuer but instead on the quality of the underlying collateral. CMOs issued directly by the FNMA and FHLMC are backed by securities which are guaranteed by those agencies. Although they are not rated, they do trade at yields that give them an AAA rating from Standard & Poor's and an Aaa rating from Moody's Investors Service. Those formed by brokerage houses which combine Fannie Maes, Freddie Macs, and Ginnie Maes for resale as CMOs are rated AAA.

However, at times some private issues may be sold. If a securities firm is the original issuer and it is not combining or using one of the three agencies (Ginnie, Freddie, or Fannie) that stand behind the issue, don't buy it!

Why Buy CMOs When You Have GNMAs?

The most serious problem of any type of mortgage security is the uncertainty of its maturity. The mortgage security is not the same as a bond that has a fixed maturity date paying the principal back only at that time. Instead, mortgage securities can mature at any time, paying small amounts at different times because of what is known as prepayment risk. For example, 20-year, 10 percent home mortgages issued for $500 million are brought together and sold as bonds by GNMA. Each month, the homeowners make their mortgage payments in which the interest and a small portion of the principal pass through to the bondholders. However, people do change locations, and as they sell their present home and pay off that mortgage, the holder of the mortgage bond will get back his or her principal sooner. Also, if interest rates were to drop substantially to 7 percent (for example) many homeowners holding these 10 percent mortgages might want to refinance their higher-costing mortgage for the new, lower rate. If this happens, the mortgage will be paid off prematurely and the holder of the mortgage bond will get back the principal in lump-sum amounts at a time when interest rates are low and there is little else to invest in. This leaves the investor with a choice of investing in the lower yield at the time or seeking riskier issues. That's not much of a choice but it can happen in a lower-interest-rate market.

The need to reduce this prepayment risk brought the CMO into being. By setting up different time periods (bond classes or tranches) each class would be able to receive its principal in sequential order. In other words, the earliest class (fast or first pay) would get all of the money repaid by the homeowners plus interest until their bond is retired. Then, the next class gets its principal back and after they are retired, the next group and the next, etc. Remember, the group that gets its money first will receive a lower yield than those who wait longer for return of their principal. Monthly checks are sent out to repay each group. If you are in the first tranche you will get both interest and repayment of principal until you are completely paid off. Those holding longer tranches will receive interest only until it is their turn and then the principal begins to move into their group.

What Other CMO Plans for Repayment Are Available?

There is a special group known as a "Z tranche" (treated as a zero coupon bond) that will not receive either principal or interest until all previous groups are paid off. These Z bonds have a stated coupon rate, but produce zero cash flow at the present time. Instead of passing the interest through cash flow, the interest accrues at the coupon rate and is added to the outstanding principal balance. You may want such a tranche because it is sold at a huge discount and offers higher yields. However, it may be many years until any cash is allocated to this group so bear that in mind when approached about this special Z tranche. Also, the interest income that is to be considered to have accrued during the year, even though you do not receive it, is taxable. In other words, you are paying taxes for money you will not receive for 15 to 30 years. However, they are an acceptable investment if placed in an IRA, Keogh or any other similar retirement plan. Individual investors holding CMOs in an IRA or Keogh account are exempt from federal and state taxes until the investor reaches retirement age or the account is prematurely terminated. Therefore, it is a good investment for executives funding their company pension plan, for individuals funding their own retirement plan, for retirees who are taking their profit sharing and rolling it over into a self-directed retirement account, and for people in low tax brackets who want a safe high-yielding bond.

Besides the uniqueness of the Z tranches, CMOs are available with a wide range of prepayment characteristics. Some of the more common are:

1. *PACs (planned amortization class):* These offer fairly predictable maturities because they protect investors against a speedup or slowdown in prepayments of mortgages.

2. *TACs (targeted amortization class):* These offer slightly less predictable maturities than PACs because they provide protection only against increasing prepayments and earlier than expected retirement. In other words, they have call protection. Their yields are accordingly slightly higher than PACs.

3. *Companions:* These tend to experience greater changes in average life than PACs and TACs. And, as you would expect, offer compensating yields of anywhere from 25 to 75 basis points (100 basis points equals 1 percent) more than PACs and TACs. If, at the present time, you have no idea as to when you wish to retire and can be flexible in your financial planning, these Companions are a way of reaching for a higher CMO yield without compromising on the security that attracted you to this investment in the first place.

If for any reason, you have to sell your CMO before your tranche ends, you have an open market to liquidate, but, as with any fixed-income security, there's an uncertainty which will depend on the number of years and the amount of the principal left in the tranche and, most important, whether interest rates are higher or lower than they were when you bought your CMO. And on the topic of risk, don't be afraid to go out on a limb because that is where the fruit is.

8

Gold, Silver, and Diamonds— Investment or Enjoyment?

The golden rule: whoever has the gold rules.

Gold has been used as money since biblical times. It has several characteristics that have made it desirable as a medium of exchange. Gold is scarce. It is durable. More than 95 percent of all the gold ever mined during the past 5000 years is still in circulation. And it is inherently valuable because of its beauty and its usefulness in industrial and decorative applications. Half a century ago the right to own gold bullion was taken away from the U.S. public, but that right was restored, in part, in 1975.

Why Is Gold Considered an Investment?

Gold has long been referred to as the "doomsday metal" because of its traditional role as a bulwark against economic, social, and political upheaval and the resulting loss of confidence in other investments, even those guaranteed by national governments. Yet this may not be true, as was seen during the stock market crash of 1987 and the terrible stock downturn in 1989, when the price of gold was expected to soar. As you may be aware, nothing occurred to its price, although the volume of sales of American Eagles (1-ounce gold coins) increased 300 percent in a single month. When Iraq invaded Kuwait on August 2, 1990, the price of gold went up only 2 percent while crude oil leaped by 27 percent. Also, look at what happened when gold hit an all-time high of $825 on January 21, 1980, and then fell only 5 days later to $634 per ounce when people realized that the world wasn't coming to an end.

The value of gold changes daily, owing to economic and political conditions. When interest rates in the United States fall, the dollar grows weaker in relation to other currencies. As a result, foreign businesspeople find U.S. investment less attractive, and some of them turn to gold instead. This forces the price of gold higher. When interest rates in the United States rise, the reverse occurs.

Let me illustrate. It was wise in the 1970s to hold gold because high interest rates coupled with a high inflation rate could not provide a real rate of return. It is obvious that if you received an interest rate of 17 percent with an inflation rate of 16 percent, your true return would be only 1 percent. Therefore, gold became an investment as a store of value. But as the inflation rate dropped over the years, gold lost must of its appeal.

Why Is Gold Considered Risky?

The value of gold is volatile. Investing in gold carries with it a definite degree of risk. Any number of events which investors cannot control can influence the price of gold. Many government actions, such as a decision by the U.S. Treasury to sell some of its vast gold holdings, can cause a sharp drop in the price of gold. Even a soaring gold price can carry risks for the investor. If the price of gold becomes prohibitively high, industrial users of the metal may turn to substitutes. This could quickly increase the supply of gold relative to demand and so force the price down. On the other hand, gold could rise because of a sudden demand. For example, if a country has "too many dollars," it may in the near future become an active participant in buying gold.

There's one more drawback to investing in gold. Gold is a non-income-producing asset. That is, it earns profits only when it is sold for a price greater than its purchase price. Gold earns no interest while it sits in your vault. Therefore, gold should be purchased as an investment only by people who have no need of current income and who have time to watch the market and sell at an advantage. This is why gold has been compared with real estate—as an investment, it is easy to get into but difficult to leave. I personally feel that it takes a lot of "brass" to speculate in gold today.

As you can see, gold is not all glitter, since it carries with it what is known as *opportunity cost.* This means that you have to give up current income that you would receive from any interest-producing asset. If this cost bothers you and you are more concerned with current income than with future gain, then gold is not the investment for you.

Despite these drawbacks, gold can be considered a good investment for some. During its strong periods, gold has been known to increase in value many times over a short span of weeks or months. And, of course, gold has a strong aesthetic and emotional appeal. Unlike most other investments, gold can serve not only as a source of security for the future, but also as an ornament to be worn today.

What Do the Numbers Mean?

Pure gold is known as *24-karat* (24K) gold. In this form, it is too soft to be made into jewelry. Therefore, it is generally mixed with other metals, such as zinc, copper, nickel, and silver, for additional strength. The number of karats marked on an item of jewelry indicates the ratio of gold to other metals contained in the piece; the higher the karat rating, the more gold the item contains (and the higher its price is likely to be). For example, 18K gold contains 18 parts gold, 6 parts other metals; 14K gold contains 14 parts gold, 10 parts other metals. This means that 14K jewelry is only 58 percent gold.

What Are the Options for Investing in Gold?

See Table 8.1 for an overview of the types of gold investments discussed below.

Gold bullion When you buy gold bullion (that from Engelhard and from Johnson-Matthey is the most widely traded), you are buying gold in the form of bars that are 99.9 percent pure gold. You can actually take physical possession of the gold bars, or you can buy gold through a bank or broker that stores the gold in its own secure facilities. Although you can buy as little as an ounce of gold bullion, a minimum of 10 ounces is usually required, with a kilo bar (32.15 ounces) being the standard. When you buy gold bullion from metal brokers, you must pay certain charges (2 to 4 percent over the spot price) apart from the ounce-for-ounce value of the gold. In addition, some banks may charge a storage fee as high as 1 percent of its value per month for holding your gold. If you have gold bullion stored by a bank or broker, make certain that it is in a totally "nonfungible" storage program. This means that your gold is not combined with the assets of others but rather held separately and labeled with your name. Under such an arrangement, you have legal title to the gold, and it cannot be considered part of the assets of the bank or dealer which could be tied up by creditors in case of a liquidation.

Gold coins: Coins are a popular form for the purchase of gold. They are not only valuable but attractive, and since they are small and portable, they can be kept in a safe in your home or in any bank vault. Most gold coins are minted to weigh 1 ounce, but some weighing as little as 0.1 ounce are available. Expect to pay between 4 and 17 percent beyond the value of the gold to cover the expense of minting and retail costs. Popular foreign gold coins include the Kruggerand, produced in South Africa, the Corona (Australia), the Panda

Table 8.1. TYPES OF GOLD INVESTMENTS

	Bullion	Coins	Shares and Funds	Certificates
Who should invest?	Conservative investors prepared to hold large amounts of gold for years	Conservative investors who wish to own small amounts of gold	Aggressive investors	Conservative investors, particularly those interested in buying at regular intervals
Where to purchase?	Large banks, coin dealers, stockbrokers	Most banks, stockbrokers, coin dealers	Stockbrokers, financial planners, by mail from no-load and low-load funds	Brokers, large banks, and Deak International
What is the smallest investment?	Tiny bars weighing 1 gram (0.032 ounce); more typically, 1 ounce, 10 ounces, and 1 kilogram (32.15 ounces)	0.1-ounce coin, more typically 1-ounce	The price of one share of an individual company; usually $250 in a mutual fund	$250 in systematic buying programs that let you subsequently invest as little as $100 a month
Advantages	Low markup on large bars (2 to 3 percent)	Ease of buying and selling; portability	Maximum gains when gold prices rise; possible dividend income; no storage costs; diversification and professional management in funds; ease of buying and selling	Low dealer markup (3 to 3.5 percent)
Disadvantages	Cost of storage (usually in a bank vault) and insurance; cost of selling	Higher markup than on bars based on minting charges; cost of storage and insurance (about $7 a year for each coin)	Maximum losses when gold prices fall; risk of loss if a mine becomes unprofitable or because of political unrest (South Africa)	Annual storage fee

(China), the gold peso (Mexico), the Maple Leaf (Canada), and, of course, the American Eagle. It is important to note that the Eagle is the only type of gold investment that may be used in an individual retirement account (IRA).

Gold stocks: These are shares in companies whose business is gold mining. The purchase of gold stocks is a way of betting on the future price of gold without actually dealing in the metal itself. Gold stocks have some advantages over owning gold directly. Securities are more liquid than the metal, and no assaying or storage costs are involved. However, shares in gold-mining companies are "leveraged instruments." That is, the value of the stock is affected disproportionately by the value of the product being sold. When the value of gold rises, the value of the stock rises even faster, but when the value of gold falls, the value of gold stock falls faster and farther. In addition, most gold stocks pay no dividends, and when the gold originates in a foreign country, it may be subject to international risks. Stay away from gold-mining stocks that purport to return riches quickly. If you want to "double your money," the safest way is to fold it and put it into your pocket!

Gold certificates: If you want to buy a small amount of gold (minimum $2500) and do not want to take delivery, certain banks and brokers will allow you to make a purchase and receive a certificate of ownership rather than the gold itself. In essence, you are buying title to gold held at a bank or broker on your behalf. A yearly fee of about 0.5 percent is usually charged. The main advantage of this way of buying gold is that you do not need to have the gold assayed when you decide to sell it. This makes your assets more liquid.

What Is the Relation between Gold and Silver?

Is *silver* (the poor person's gold) a better investment as a precious metal? Where as gold's primary role is monetary, silver's is industrial. Silver has many more commercial uses than gold—Kodak, for example, uses large amounts of silver every year in manufacturing photographic film—and because of the unique physical and chemical properties of silver, no substitute seems likely to be devised. These industrial uses provide a solid foundation for the future value of silver.

The ratio of the price of gold to the price of silver is a useful investment guideline for those interested in buying either of these metals. You can easily determine the current gold/silver ratio by dividing the morning's gold price by that of silver. In past years, the average gold/silver ratio has been 32:1. A high or low gold/silver ratio indicates that one of the metals is currently undervalued in relation to the other, and you will want to consider moving your holdings into the undervalued metal. For example, a gold/silver ratio of 50:1 shows that silver is undervalued and therefore the metal to buy. A ratio of 15:1 means "buy gold." Remember that this ratio is only a basic guideline and certainly does not apply in all economic environments, especially today.

How Do You Purchase Silver for Investment Purposes?

As with gold, there are several ways to buy silver. One way is to buy junk silver, which consists of a bag of pre-1965 U.S. dimes, quarters, or half dollars with a face value of $1000 and a market value based on the price of silver for the day. Silver bullion is available in 1000-ounce bars, while silver certificates are receipts for the purchase of silver, held at a bank in your name. Like gold certificates, silver certificates have the advantages of being highly liquid and posing no storage or security problems, so your wealth will remain intact.

How Do Diamonds Compare with Gold in Today's Economy?

Even though diamonds have been considered a risk investment, with today's poor economy forcing people to sell their precious stones at any acceptable price, you can find many good bargains if you know what you are doing. A *diamond*, it has been said, is nothing more than a piece of coal that has made good under pressure. As an investment it has a great deal in common with gold. Both gold and diamonds tend to be costly in terms of brokers' fees and sales markups, but each offers the investor safety as a hedge against inflation. Diamonds are also a good hedge against depression. Have you noticed what happens when you give a diamond to a depressed spouse?

For people with substantial wealth who wish to concentrate a lot of that wealth in a small space, diamonds can be a sound investment. Unlike gold, diamonds don't demand continual monitoring of a highly volatile market; diamond prices don't fluctuate widely.

How Do You Purchase Diamonds?

If you do decide to buy diamonds as an investment, regard it as a long-term proposal, not a get-rich-quick scheme. Buy gems weighing from 1 to 3 carats and have them evaluated by an appraiser from the Gemological Institute of American (GIA). Once you receive your diamond's GIA certificate, you can easily determine the stone's fair price by consulting a grading table, since the certificate will state the "four C's": color, cut, clarity, and carat.

Color refers to how white or yellow a diamond is. The color of a diamond is rated alphabetically from D to Z. The closer a diamond is to the D grade, the whiter its color and the more valuable the stone. *Cut* refers to the shape of the diamond and the skill with which it has been crafted. The brilliance and beauty of a diamond depend largely on how accurately the diamond-cutter did his or her job. Note that round diamonds are generally the most stable. *Clarity* refers to the number and size of the flaws (or "inclusions") contained in the stone. It takes an expert with a magnifying glass to rate the clarity of a stone. Diamonds range from internally flawless (IF) to imperfect (I-3). *Carat* is the unit of weight for the gem, with 1 carat equaling 200 milligrams ($\frac{1}{142}$ ounce). The value of a diamond increases dramatically as its size increases; a 2-carat stone will usually be worth more than twice as much as a 1-carat stone of comparable quality.

What Are the Major Drawbacks to Investing in Diamonds?

1. Most diamonds appreciate in value less than 8 percent a year.
2. Like gold, diamonds are non-income-producing; no interest or dividends are paid on diamonds.
3. Diamonds are relatively difficult to liquidate.
4. The jewelry value of a diamond is much higher than its investment value because of heavy retail markups, which range from 40 to 300 percent, with 100 percent being the average. A diamond bought from a jeweler for $8000 is likely to yield only about $4000 if you decide to sell it to another jeweler later.
5. Diamonds have high storage and insurance costs.
6. About 85 percent of the world's diamond market is controlled by the DeBeers–Central Selling Organization, headquartered in London. Therefore, the price of diamonds is dependent on the activities of a single group.

How Would You Summarize Investing in Precious Metals or Gems?

Gold, silver, and diamonds probably have more drawbacks than advantages as investment options for the average middle-income American. If you want to try your hand at investing in them, go ahead; if you have educated yourself and follow the market carefully, you may do very well. But most people will probably derive more benefit and happiness from the beauty and sentimental value of gold, silver, and diamond objects than they will from their investment value. And on the topic of happiness, the secret to being happy is to count your blessings while others are adding up their troubles.

9

Life Insurance—
The Risk Protector

For 3 days after death, hair and fingernails
continue to grow but phone calls do taper off.

What Is the Purpose of Life Insurance?

The basic purpose of life insurance is to offer financial protection to your loved ones in the event of your death. The benefit it provides is one which you hope you won't need—at least not soon—but which most people would be foolish to do without. Remember that:

1. Life insurance is usually the major source of liquidity to beneficiaries.

2. Life insurance proceeds, in most states, are exempt from the claims of the deceased's creditors.

3. Life insurance proceeds are usually not subject to probate, thus eliminating both probate expenses and probate delays.

Because beneficiaries avoid probate and receive the face value of the policy tax-free, be certain to name contingent beneficiaries. If not, and your primary beneficiary predeceases you, the insurance proceeds of your policy upon your death will become part of your will and will end up in probate court. Also, naming young children as beneficiaries may not always be a smart move. An insurance company will not pay proceeds upon death to a minor. The money will be held until a court approved guardian is established. A needless delay!

Speaking of children, I do not believe in life insurance for children. If your son or daughter is a famous movie or rock star, bringing into the family huge sums of money, then I can accept the notion of insurance. But if your child is just a normal kid, you don't need it. If you are told that the money could be used for final expenses in case of the death of the youngster, the $3000–$5000 may be a slight hardship but not the reason for such a purchase. If a salesperson touts you on the concept of using such a policy as a method of saving for the child's college education, you would be far better off with most other financial instruments that do not charge for the added expenses of mortality (life insurance costs) and commissions. Stay away.

Many life insurance policies contain investment features which can be used to provide additional income for you and your family. You probably won't want to buy life insurance primarily for its investment value—other forms of investments are generally more lucrative—but the investment benefits can be a significant secondary reason for buying insurance, as well as a factor in choosing among the available policies. So it pays to understand the different types of life insurance and their varying values as investments.

Let's consider the most popular forms of life insurance today; with special attention to their investment potential: (1) term insurance, (2) straight life insurance, and (3) universal life insurance. Table 9.1 provides a summary.

How Does Term Insurance Work?

Term life insurance offers the greatest amount of financial protection at the lowest cost in premiums. This is because when you buy term insurance, you buy the possible death benefit only; there is no savings or investment of a specified

Table 9.1. SUMMARY OF LIFE INSURANCE PROGRAMS			
Type of insurance program			
Feature	Term	Whole life	Universal life
Premium	Lowest cost; increases in cost at the end of each term	Fixed premium; reinvestment of interest reduces payments insured for life	Flexible premiums; insured for specified period
Cash value	None	Some cash value	Varies with amount invested
Objectives	Protection for a limited time period to cover specific and temporary risks	Protection for life with cash value for insured	Life insurance protection plus high rate of return on savings component

sum if you die during the life of the policy (the "term" from which this type of insurance gets its name). Term policies are usually issued for a specific period of years, after which the insurance coverage can be renewed but only at a higher premium rate.

Two variations on the term insurance policy are the *decreasing term* policy, in which the premiums remain the same but the amount of the death benefits decreases as you get older, and the *level term* policy, in which the amount of the death benefit remains the same but the size of the premium increases over time.

Term insurance is popular in instances where the need for life insurance protection is temporary or where other, more costly forms of insurance protection is temporary or where other, more costly forms of insurance are unaffordable. For example, term insurance may be an ideal choice for a young family with children, where insurance protection is vital but the family income may still be modest. As the family grows older and the parents' careers take wing, the family income will probably increase, and other types of policies may become more attractive. But remember this: Although the premiums of term will eventually become more expensive than cash-value policies mentioned in the next few pages, term has the advantage of being far less costly at the time in people's lives when large amounts of coverage are most needed.

How Does Straight Life Insurance Work?

Also known as *whole life insurance,* a straight life policy offers a specified death benefit (the face value of the policy) in exchange for an unchanging premium payment. The size of the premium depends mainly on your age at the time you purchase the policy; the younger you are, the lower your annual premium will be. At the time of your death, the face value of the policy will be paid to your beneficiary.

Unlike term insurance, straight life insurance includes an investment feature. Part of your premium payment is placed in a savings fund and invested by the insurance company. As the years pass, the amount of money in this fund will grow, both from your contributions and from the company's investment earnings. This growing sum is known as the policy's *cash surrender value.* It is quite small at first but, after a number of years, can become a substantial amount of money. The cash surrender value of your policy can benefit you in two ways. First, if you terminate the policy, you can receive the cash surrender value as a lump sum (unlike term insurance, in which you walk away with nothing). Second, while the policy is in force, you can borrow against the cash surrender value at a favorable interest rate, even if you may not qualify for other types of loans. This provision can be useful, for example, when college tuition bills come due.

The investment value of straight life insurance gives it an advantage over term insurance. However, it is considerably more costly. The amount of savings you'll accumulate through your insurance policy is probably smaller than the amount you could save through other investment plans. And, of course, in order for your beneficiary to receive the death benefit, you must continue to pay premiums until you die. This can be a financial strain, especially for older people whose earnings have fallen after retirement. So consider the pros and cons carefully before opting for a straight life policy.

Another factor to consider is the term *cost*. This is the difference between what you pay in premiums and what you will get back. If you buy term insurance, you will pay a premium and get nothing back; thus your cost for insuring your life is the premium. If there is a cash surrender value, as in the other types of life insurance, your cost is smaller than the premium. Cost can also be reduced by dividends in the "participating" policies, but not all policies carry this feature. Thus, in order to evaluate the costs of different policies, you need to compare the premiums, cash surrender values, and dividends, if any. Cost indexes encompassing one or more of these factors are available from your insurance representative or from the company itself. These indexes give you an accurate method of assessing the relative costs of similar policies. All you need do is compare the index number given for each policy. The lower the cost index number, the less the policy will cost you. It's as simple as that.

How Does Universal Life Insurance Work?

Because of much criticism about insurance companies' low returns on whole life policies, the concept of *universal life insurance* was born. Unlike deferred annuities, the universal life policy is bought mainly for its insurance feature. It was first introduced in 1979 as a type of life insurance which combines insurance protection (in the form of term insurance coverage) with a savings plan that builds tax-deferred income at highly competitive rates. This income becomes taxable only when the policy lapses or is surrendered. The holder of a universal life policy chooses the amount of life insurance protection he or she wants, and part of the premium goes to cover that protection. The insurance company invests the rest of the premium payment in various high-yielding instruments. Watch out for these yields though. Although high, they are usually "gross" rates, meaning that administrative and other costs have not been considered in the computation. The insurance company's investment managers usually decide on the investment policy, so your growth or yield is determined by their decisions. If the managers make a series of bad investment decisions, the cash value of your policy will decline. This doesn't happen with straight life insurance, in which cash values are projected using a fixed interest rate, so that you know in advance just what your policy's cash surrender value will be at any time.

Another important feature to consider is that this type of policy is very flexible. At any time, the amount of insurance coverage can be increased or decreased, the size of the premiums can be adjusted, and the accumulated cash value can be withdrawn by means of an automatic policy loan.

An interesting option that is offered with some universal life policies, known as a *vanishing premium*, allows you to discontinue your payments after a certain period of time. Assume you are 40 years old. You will pay a larger premium for a fixed number of years (I'll use 25 years as an example). After the twenty-fifth year the earnings on the premiums will have accumulated and the premiums will be paid from the earnings. So, by the time you are ready for retirement, you no longer have to worry about paying life insurance premiums. Remember that the death benefit does not decline when you stop paying premiums.

A word about low yields and life insurance projections. Many policies bought in the 1980s had interest rates projected at 12 percent (and higher)—at that time the current rate. These projections are no longer valid, and policyholders may find that their idea of using cash surrender value to supplement their retirement income is at risk. Also, people who bought "vanishing premium" policies may discover that, because of the low yields of the early 1990s, they have to continue making premium payments long after the period of "no premiums" has expired.

One last point. If the earnings on the universal life policy are more than what the company had projected, you may find that the death benefit actually increases. The reason is that by tax law, the cash value of the policy cannot be allowed to come too close to the policy's death benefit. If this should occur, the death benefit must be increased or the policy would lose its tax-favored status.

Therefore, when you shop for universal life insurance, it's very important to compare the investment policies of different insurance companies. Some are more successful than others. Also find out about the fees charged by the companies you're considering. Some charge heavy sales commissions, which may run as high as 50 percent of your first year's premium; others charge large surrender fees (known as *back-end loads*) in the event you decide to cancel your policy. Ask before you buy.

Why Is It Important to Know about Insurance Company Ratings?

The issue of the financial strength of an insurance company to meet its obligations is a most important item for the investor to understand. The role of a rating agency is to evaluate an insurance company's financial position and its ability to pay policyholder claims. Insurance customers and prospective customers can benefit greatly from seeing these valuative ratings so that they can compare one company with another. Thus the reader can better determine which companies possess the stability and financial resources needed in today's economy and then select the best company according to its product, its service, and its performance. The three leading independent analysts are A. M. Best, Standard & Poor's and Moody's. Although they have

common characteristics in their evaluations, adopt the
same accounting methods, and issue letter grades (including the use of modifiers), their rating methodologies differ.
Each has its own basic approach to evaluating the data and

Table 9.2. INSURANCE COMPANY RATINGS			
Description	A. M. Best	S&P	Moody's
Superior Smallest degree of risk	A+	AAA	Aaa
Excellent Capacity to meet obligations differs only slightly from highest-rated category	A+(c) A, A(c) A −	AA+ AA AA −	Aa1 Aa2 Aa3
Good Strong financial security, but somewhat more susceptible to adverse changes in the economy	A − (c) B+ B+(c)	A+ A A −	A1 A2 A3
Adequate Financially secure, but may beat risk in the future	B B(c) B −	BBB+ BBB BBB −	Baa1 Baa2 Baa3
Below average Judged to have speculative elements	B − (c) C+ C+(c)	BB+ BB BB −	Ba1 Ba2 Ba3
Financially weak High vulnerability to adverse economic conditions	C C(c) C −	B+ B B −	B1 B2 B3
Nonviable Ability to meet obligations is highly questionable		CCC CC, D	Caa Ca, C

(c) = Best's contingency rating, indicating it sees a temporary decline in
profitability or liquidity.

performance of insurance companies. Table 9.2 provides a summary.

Information can be obtained by calling these firms directly:

Standard & Poor's (212) 208-1527

Moody's (212) 553-0377

A. M. Best (900) 555-2378

Also, you can turn directly to your state's department of insurance. If you are interested in information on the solvency of a life insurance company doing business in your state, call or write to the addresses listed in Table 9.3.

What Other Types of Insurance Policies or Options Are Available?

Although an enormous array of choices exist, the "Second to Die" policy and the accelerated death benefit (ADB) option should be mentioned.

Under the 1981 Economic Recovery Tax Act, an unlimited federal marital deduction was allowed at the first death. That meant that all federal estate tax payments would not be levied until the death of the surviving spouse. This was not always the case. Prior to 1981, estate taxes were levied on 50 percent of the assets left to the surviving spouse—an immediate tax. A new type of insurance arose from this procedure. Known as the "second to die" policy, it is used primarily for paying estate taxes, adding to a lowering inheritance, reducing insurance premiums, and caring for children with special problems. The concept works in this way. Instead of one policy on one spouse's life or one policy on each spouse, there is one policy insuring both lives payable at the death of the second insured. It is much cheaper than having two policies and more efficient. However, there are certain disadvantages to such a policy. Income may be needed immediately after the death of the first insured, especially if there are large debts to be paid.

Table 9.3. STATE SOURCES OF INSURANCE INFORMATION

State	Address	Telephone
Alabama	135 S. Union St., Montgomery 36130	(205) 269-3550
Alaska	C St., Suite 740, Anchorage 99503	(907) 562-3626
Arizona	3030 N. Third St., Phoenix 85012	(602) 255-5400
Arkansas	400 University Tower Bldg., Little Rock 72204	(501) 371-1325
California	770 L St., Sacramento 95814	(800) 927-4357
Colorado	303 W. Colfax Ave., Suite 500, Denver 80204	(303) 866-6400
Connecticut	P.O.Box 816, Hartford 06142	(203) 297-3800
Delaware	841 Silver Lake Blvd., Dover 19901	(800) 282-8611
District of Columbia	P.O. Box 37200, 20013	(202) 727-8000
Florida	State Capitol, PL-11, Tallahassee 32399	(800) 342-2762
Georgia	2 Martin Luther King Jr. Dr., Atlanta 30334	(404) 656-2056
Hawaii	P.O. Box 3614, Honolulu 96811	(800) 468-4644
Idaho	500 S. 10th St., Boise 83720	(208) 334-2250
Illinois	320 W. Washington St., Springfield 62767	(217) 782-4515
Indiana	311 W. Washington St., Indianapolis 46204	(800) 622-4461
Iowa	Lucas State Office Bldg., Des Moines 50319	(515) 281-5705
Kansas	420 S.W. Ninth St., Topeka 66612	(800) 432-2484
Kentucky	P.O. Box 5175, Frankfort 40602	(502) 564-3630
Louisiana	P.O. Box 94214, Baton Rouge 70804	(504) 342-5301
Maine	State House, Station 34, Augusta 04333	(207) 582-8707
Maryland	501 St. Paul Place, Baltimore 21202	(800) 492-7521
Massachusetts	280 Friend St.,Boston 02114	(617) 727-7189
Michigan	P.O. Box 30220, Lansing 48909	(517) 373-0240
Minnesota	133 E. Seventh St., St. Paul 55101	(800) 652-9747
Mississippi	1804 Walter Sillers Bldg., Jackson 39201	(800) 562-2957
Missouri	P.O. Box 690, Jefferson City 65101	(800) 726-7390
Montana	126 N. Sanders St., Helena 59620	(406) 444-2040
Nebraska	941 O St., Lincoln 68508	(402) 471-2201
Nevada	1665 Hot Springs Rd., Carson City 89710	(800) 992-0900
New Hampshire	169 Manchester St., Concord 03301	(800) 852-3416

Table 9.3. STATE SOURCES OF INSURANCE INFORMATION (Continued)

State	Address	Telephone
New Jersey	20 W. State St., CN 325, Trenton 08625	(609) 292-5360
New Mexico	P.O. Drawer 1269, Santa Fe 87504	(505) 827-4500
New York	160 W. Broadway, New York 10013	(800) 342-3736
North Carolina	P.O. Box 26387, Raleigh 27611	(800) 662-7777
North Dakota	Capitol Bldg., 600 East Blvd., Bismarck 58505	(800) 247-0560
Ohio	2100 Stella Court, Columbus 43266	(800) 686-1526
Oklahoma	P.O. Box 53408, Oklahoma City 73152	(800) 522-0071
Oregon	21 Labor and Industries Bldg., Salem 97310	(503) 378-4271
Pennsylvania	1326 Strawberry Square, Harrisburg 17120	(717) 787-5173
Rhode Island	233 Richmond St., Providence 02903	(401) 277-2223
South Carolina	P.O. Box 100105, Columbia 29202	(800) 768-3467
South Dakota	910 E. Sioux Ave., Pierre 57501	(605) 773-3563
Tennessee	500 James Robertson Pkwy., Nashville 37243	(800) 342-4029
Texas	1110 San Jacinto Blvd., Austin 78701	(800) 252-3439
Utah	3110 State Office Bldg., Salt Lake City 84114	(801) 538-3800
Vermont	120 State St., Montpelier 05620	(802) 828-3301
Virginia	P.O. Box 1157, Richmond 23209	(800) 552-7945
Washington	Insurance Bldg. AQ-21, Olympia 98504	(800) 562-6900
West Virginia	2019 Washington St. East, Charleston 25305	(800) 642-9004
Wisconsin	121 E. Wilson St., Madison 53702	(800) 236-8517
Wyoming	122 W. 25th St., Cheyenne 82002	(307) 777-7401

Also, in the light of so many second marriages, individuals may want to leave their estate directly to their children and not to the surviving spouse. I recommend strongly that before you sign up for a "second to die" policy, you speak to your attorney.

A new life insurance feature being offered is the ADB (accelerated death benefit) option. What it means is that if the insured becomes terminally ill (life expectancy of 6 months to 1 year) and needs funds quickly, he or she can receive money from the death benefit while living and use the money as he or she sees fit. It is a wonderful idea for freeing up funds to make the last days of terminally ill insureds more meaningful. The disadvantage of such a policy option is its cost. Surcharges may run as high as 15 percent of the basic premium, and severe medical restrictions do apply.

What Should You Remember about Choosing a Policy?

On the basis of the brief descriptions in this chapter, if you consider your objectives, you will now be able to choose the best type of policy for you. Term insurance is your choice if your needs require large amounts of insurance and you cannot afford cash value policies. Consider straight life or universal life only if you can afford the higher premiums. Remember that you should not forsake important coverage for investment yield. Also, the tax-deferred features of the investment-type policies are of most benefit to people in high tax brackets. If you are not in a higher tax bracket, you may be better off in a taxable investment paying a higher rate even though the interest is subject to tax.

If a policy is lost, you can send a self-addressed stamped envelope to The American Council of Life Insurance, 1001 Pennsylvania Avenue, NW, Washington, DC 20004 and request a "policy search form." And on the topic of life insurance, as the insurance agent said, "Don't let me push you into making a hasty decision. Sleep on it tonight. If you should wake up tomorrow, let me know what you've decided."

10

Money Market Accounts— The Parking Lot

The idea is to make a little money first and then to make a little money last.

As far as I am concerned, the money market is nothing more than a parking lot, a temporary area for buying and selling high-yield, short-term instruments of credit. In the money market, securities such as Treasury bills, certificates of deposit (CDs), and short-term commercial loans are bought and sold. Since these securities carry high interest rates, they make money grow quickly. But they normally require extremely large investments (Treasury bills, $10,000; jumbo CDs and commercial paper, $100,000) that only wealthy individuals or large institutions can afford. That's where money market funds come in. First made available in 1974, money market funds offer the small investor a chance to take advantage of the interest rates prevailing in the money markets by pooling many people's money.

How Does a Money Market Account Work?

Money market funds operate by combining many small investors' funds to accumulate the kind of money needed to buy costly money market instruments (jumbo CDs, Treasury bills, etc). Since the instruments purchased by the fund have different maturities, the fund earns interest on a daily basis. Each investor receives his or her share of the interest by means of a regular statement, usually issued monthly. The amount earned on an investment varies continually as the prevalent interest rates in the money market rise and fall.

Money market funds are managed by investment firms and brokerage houses; the management fee is deducted from the fund's earnings. Usually no redemption charges are imposed on the fund. Most firms transact business by mail, so a money market fund headquartered in Illinois, for example, may have shareholders in any of the 50 states. A minimum deposit is required to open a money market account; $1000 is typical. You can add to your investment at any time, and your funds are completely liquid—you can make withdrawals whenever you wish. Many money market funds allow you to withdraw your money simply by writing a check, although there is usually a limit on the number of checks that you are permitted to write (five checks per month, for example). Thus you may want to consider using a money market fund in place of a conventional checking account, which earns you no interest.

What Types of Money Market Funds Are Offered?

Money market funds can be broken into three categories, based upon the type of instruments in which the funds invest.

1. *General money market funds:* These invest primarily in nongovernmental securities, such as bank certificates of deposit, commercial loans, and banker's acceptances. Of the three types of funds, general money market funds usually pay the highest interest rates.

2. *Government-only money market funds:* These invest only in securities issued by the U.S. government or by a federal agency. Such funds boast a somewhat higher degree of safety than the general money market funds, but they pay a little less.

3. *Tax-free money market funds:* These purchase only short-term, tax-exempt municipal bonds and are especially suitable for investors in high tax brackets. Although this type of money market fund is exempt from federal tax, it could still be subject to state and local income taxes, since most states do not exempt taxes on municipals issued out of state. The exceptions are Alaska, Florida, Indiana, Nebraska, New Mexico, South Dakota, Utah, Vermont, Washington, Wyoming, and the District of Columbia. If you reside in a high-income-tax state, search out those municipal money market funds that purchase investments only within your state of residence. For example, a fund may obtain only Massachusetts securities so that all the income earned will be "triple tax-free" to Massachusetts investors. However, Illinois, Iowa, Kansas, Oklahoma and Wisconsin will impose a tax on municipal bonds issued within their state.

Another important point about this type of investment: Because of the liquidity of a money market fund, it is an ideal way to invest idle cash that might otherwise find its way into a low-paying passbook savings account. For example, placing the proceeds from the sale of securities into a money market fund until you've decided upon your next investment venture is a good way of earning continuous high interest on your money. Also, many money market funds are part of a larger group of other types of funds (known as a *family of funds*) that permit you to move your money from one investment to another as financial conditions change. The most prominent funds are listed daily in the financial sections of newspapers. These listings show the average maturity (the shorter the time, the faster the fund reacts to changes in interest rates) and the average yield for the previous 7 days.

How Do Money Markets Issued by Banks Work?

Banks entered the money market field in 1982 with their version of the money market fund: the *money market deposit account* (MMDA). The MMDA was authorized by Congress in order to stem the $200 billion tide of withdrawals that banks claimed had been lured away by money market funds. Yet you do not hear much about MMDAs, since they are not adequately advertised. You see, the banks would rather you purchase their CDs, because with CDs they will have your money for a longer period of time.

The MMDA is similar in many ways to the money market fund. It too is based on the pooling concept, allowing small investors to earn interest rates otherwise reserved for large institutional investors or wealthy individuals. Like a money market fund, an MMDA requires a minimum initial deposit as well as a minimum balance. However, as of 1986 federal regulations no longer mandated a minimum MMDA balance. Thus banks became free to enforce a minimum balance rule at their discretion, so don't blame the government if your bank requires a high minimum balance.

Finally, as with a money market fund, an MMDA is a good way to invest cash for a short period.

What Are the Major Differences between the Money Market Fund and the MMDA?

When you invest in a money market fund, you become a shareholder in the fund. You and the other shareholders receive all the income earned by the fund's investments, less a small management fee (usually about 0.5 percent annually). When you invest in an MMDA, on the other hand, you are not a shareholder but simply a depositor. Investors in MMDAs do not necessarily receive all the interest generated by their investments, but receive whatever interest rate the bank chooses to pay. Furthermore, the bank is free to invest your money any way it sees fit, even in investments that have little or nothing to do with the money market. Therefore, you have no guarantee that the interest rate you receive will truly reflect the money market rate.

Note, too, the difference in the way the money market funds and the MMDAs usually advertise the interest rates they pay. Money market funds normally advertise the current simple interest rate being earned by the fund. This yield, which is not guaranteed, can change daily as conditions in the money markets change. By contrast, banks often promote MMDAs by advertising the effective yield rate, which is usually a fraction of a point higher than the simple interest rate because of compounding. However, the effective yield rate can be misleading, since it assumes that the bank will be giving compound interest on an unchanging interest rate for a full year. Since this is highly unlikely to occur, you should take with a grain of salt the high effective yields claimed by banks.

Therefore, these lower-yielding instruments will lag behind those with shorter maturities and thus could cause a loss in the fund's market value. The average maturity for investments held by general money market funds is about 35 days; for the tax-free funds, about 65 days.

There are other differences between money market funds and MMDAs to consider:

1. With an MMDA, you have a person-to-person relationship with a bank officer whom you know, in contrast to the rather anonymous, through-the-mail relationship usually offered by the money market funds. For some investors, dealing with a personal banker is psychologically important.

2. The money market fund may be preferable if you plan on making frequent withdrawals from your account. You are usually permitted unlimited withdrawals by check from the fund. With an MMDA, there is normally a limit of three checks per month. However, in most banks you can make deposits or withdrawals 24 hours a day by

means of the bank's automated teller machines (ATMs). You cannot do this with the money market fund.

3. With an MMDA, you may lose up to a month's interest if you close out your account anytime within a given month. With a money market fund, this cannot happen because of daily payments of interest.

Are Both the Money Market Fund and the MMDA Safe Investments?

As with any form of investment, safety is a factor to consider. Your investment in an MMDA offered by a bank or a savings and loan institution is insured by the federal government up to a maximum of $100,000. If safety is of overriding importance to you, choose an MMDA over a money market fund. However, you should realize that the money market funds have an excellent safety track record. This is because they invest only in short-term instruments issued by such secure institutions as government agencies, large corporations, and major banks. An investor's rule of thumb is that the shorter the maturity of an investment, the lower the risk. Why is this? If interest rates should rise rapidly, funds holding long-term maturities would find it more difficult to liquidate their low-yielding holdings. Furthermore, the Securities and Exchange Commission (SEC) regulates money market funds very strictly.

Therefore, the concept of the money market is simple:

1. The principal you invest is safe.

2. You can withdraw your money at any time with no penalty.

3. You'll earn interest rates that reflect up-to-date market conditions.

This combination of benefits makes money market investing one of today's most popular options. And on the topic of investing, remember that if you hit the ball over the fence, you can take your time going around the bases.

11

Mortgages— The Finances of Home Ownership

Love your neighbor—but don't pull down the fences.

For most people, buying a home entails taking out a mortgage to help meet the cost of purchase. You are normally required to pay a percentage of the purchase price in cash; this is called the *down payment*. The remainder of the purchase price is covered by the mortgage, with your title to the house used as security for the unpaid balance on your mortgage. This means that if you are unable to repay your mortgage, the lender has the right to foreclose—that is, to take possession of the property. Most mortgage loans are made by banks and savings and loan associations, though other institutions and individuals may sometimes offer mortgages.

What Must You Know about a Mortgage?

There are four terms that are essential in understanding mortgages.

1. *Origination fee:* This is a one-time charge that the lender will add as a cost of the mortgage.

2. *Simple interest rate:* This is the quoted rate of the loan. If a mortgage is negotiated for 15 years at 8 percent with a 3 point origination fee, the simple interest is still 8 percent.

3. *Effective interest rate:* This is different from the simple rate in that it is the actual cost of borrowing after considering origination fees. In the preceding example the effective rate would be 8.2 percent.

4. *PITI:* This stands for the total monthly payment of principal, interest, taxes, and insurance that is so important to know when a family budgets for the purchase of a home.

What Types of Mortgages Are Offered?

Many mortgages provide for repayment over a 10- to 30-year period in equal monthly payment amounts based on a fixed rate of interest. Each payment includes both repayment of principal and payment of interest, with early payments representing interest and later payments representing mainly principal. This is known as the fixed-rate mortgage payment. However, the volatile economic climate of the late 1970s—in particular, soaring interest rates—led to the increased use of another type of mortgage, the *adjustable-rate mortgage* (ARM). This type of mortgage is usually a long-term loan, providing for repayment in 20 to 30 years. It differs from the traditional fixed-rate mortgage in that the interest rate on the loan changes at stated intervals. Thus, as interest rates rise, the amount you must pay the bank each month rises too; as interest rates fall, so do your monthly payments.

How Does the ARM Work?

The amount you must pay each month on an adjustable-rate mortgage loan depends on three factors:

1. *Interval:* The period of time between adjustments of the interest rate. Typical intervals are 6 months and 1 year.

2. *Index:* A guideline used in determining the current interest rate on the mortgage. The index will be clearly defined at the time the mortgage is made. Any of a number of widely accepted financial guidelines may be used as an index; one typical index is the current interest rate on 6-month U.S. Treasury bills. As the index goes up or down, so does the interest rate on your mortgage, and along with it your monthly payment.

3. *Cap:* A predetermined figure limiting the movement of the interest rate on your mortgage in any single interval. If an adjustable-rate mortgage includes a cap, and not all do, the interest rate may not change by an amount greater than the cap, even though the variation in the index would normally call for a greater change.

As you can see, an adjustable-rate mortgage has one major disadvantage for the borrower: It's impossible to know beforehand how large your monthly payments will be in the future. Thus much of the security of the traditional fixed-rate mortgage is forfeited. In many cases, an adjustable-rate mortgage is offered at a lower initial interest rate than a comparable fixed-rate mortgage, but you won't know how long this advantage will last. Therefore, it is better for most home buyers to obtain (for their peace of mind) the fixed-rate mortgage.

What Are the Basic Requirements for a Mortgage?

Lenders usually require that your housing costs do not exceed 28 percent of your family gross income. When you add to the 28 percent your fixed payments for auto, credit cards, loans, and the like, your total fixed debt should not be more than 36 percent of gross monthly income. Also, do not attempt to secure a mortgage whose cost will be more than $2\frac{1}{2}$ times your annual income. A $70,000 annual family income is just enough to purchase a home with a mortgage of $175,000.

Table 11.1 provides some guidelines.

Table 11.1. HOW MUCH MORTGAGE YOU CAN CARRY		
Gross annual income	Maximum monthly PITI	
	28%	36%
$40,000	$933	$1200
45,000	1050	1350
50,000	1167	1500
55,000	1283	1650
60,000	1400	1800
65,000	1516	1980
70,000	1633	2100
75,000	1750	2250
80,000	1867	2400
85,000	1983	2550
90,000	2100	2700
95,000	2216	2850
100,000	2333	3000
125,000	2916	3750
150,000	3500	4500
175,000	4083	5250
200,000	4666	6000

How Does Refinancing a Mortgage Work in Today's Market?

When possible, it may be advantageous for you to switch mortgage methods by refinancing if interest rates go down. But it is not always true that a lower interest rate alone means that refinancing is the way to go. For example, it could take many years to recoup the cost of the up-front fees, which could include lawyer's fees, title search and insurance, recording taxes, and, possibly, bank origination fees. In comparing figures, you must also consider the tax consequences before any refinancing decision can take place. Remember, by reducing your mortgage payment (which includes tax-deductible interest), you reduce the only tax deduction for interest which is left for the middle-income investor. This then raises your taxable income. So think carefully and weigh all the factors necessary to make an intelligent choice. As a rule of thumb, do not refinance your existing mortgage unless you can benefit by at least 2 percentage points off the old mortgage rate.

Table 11.2 gives the monthly mortgage payments under a fixed-rate mortgage. For example, a $75,000 mortgage at 8 percent for 15 years would be calculated as follows:

1. Look across the 8 percent line to the column titled 15 years.

2. The amount is $9.56.

3. Multiply the $9.56 by 75 (represents $75,000).

4. The result is $717 monthly payment.

A $100,000 mortgage would be computed as $9.56 × 100 = $956.

A further consideration, however, is pretax versus aftertax money. Assume that you have a 30-year, 10 percent, $100,000 mortgage that you will refinance at 7.5 percent. According to Table 11.2, your present monthly mortgage payment would be $878 (10 percent) while your new refinanced monthly payment would be only $700 (7.5 percent). You would consider that it would be a monthly savings of $178 ($878 − 700), but that is based upon pretax money. In order for you to get your aftertax savings, you must multiply your tax bracket rate (e.g., 28 percent) by the pretax savings ($178) and then subtract:

$$
\begin{array}{ll}
\$178 & \text{Pretax savings} \\
\underline{-\ 50} & (\$178 \times .28, \text{rounded off}) \\
\underline{\$128} & \text{Aftertax savings}
\end{array}
$$

Table 11.2. MONTHLY MORTGAGE PAYMENTS FOR EACH $1000 OWED

Interest rate (%)	Years				
	10	15	20	25	30
6.00	$11.11	$8.44	$7.17	$6.45	$6.00
6.25	11.23	8.58	7.31	6.60	6.16
6.50	11.36	8.72	7.46	6.76	6.33
6.75	11.49	8.85	7.61	6.91	6.49
7.00	11.62	8.99	7.76	7.07	6.63
7.25	11.75	9.13	7.91	7.23	6.83
7.50	11.88	9.28	8.06	7.39	7.00
7.75	12.01	9.42	8.21	7.56	7.17
8.00	12.14	9.56	8.37	7.72	7.34
8.25	12.27	9.71	8.53	7.89	7.52
8.50	12.40	9.85	8.68	8.06	7.69
8.75	12.54	10.00	8.84	8.23	7.87
9.00	12.67	10.15	9.00	8.40	8.05
9.50	12.94	10.45	9.33	8.74	8.41
10.00	13.22	10.75	9.66	9.09	8.78
10.50	13.50	11.06	9.99	9.45	9.14
11.00	13.78	11.37	10.33	9.81	9.51
11.50	14.06	11.69	10.67	10.17	9.90
12.00	14.35	12.01	11.02	10.54	10.28

What Are the Tax Considerations in Mortgage Financing?

No matter which type of mortgage you obtain, you'll receive significant tax benefits during the repayment period. These benefits arise from the fact that interest payments on the original purchase of a home, up to $1 million, are deductible from your taxable income for federal income tax purposes. For most homeowners, that's a substantial amount.

If you're currently shopping for a home (and a mortgage), you should be aware of two other factors which will affect the cost of home buying: closing costs and points.

Closing costs are one-time expenses that include the cost of a title search, title insurance, surveying fees, attorneys' fees, mortgage recording tax, and many other smaller fees that can total as much as 5 percent of the value of the home you're buying. Before purchase, you should receive from the lending institution a good-faith estimate of what your closing costs will be.

Points are one-time lump-sum charges levied by the bank at the time you buy your home. A point is 1 percent of the total amount of the loan; the bank may charge from 2 to 4 points. For example, if you take out a $60,000 mortgage from a bank which charges 4 points for the loan, you will have to pay the bank a $2400 fee at the time of purchase. To receive the most for your money, you should estimate how long you intend to own the home. Then decide on the best combination of interest rate and points. Because points are an up-front fee, whether you sell your house and pay off the loan after only 15 years or 30 years, remember that the longer you hold the loan, the smaller the impact the points will have on the effective rate of mortgage. Try this three-step comparison approach:

1. Estimate how long you intend to keep the loan.

2. Divide that period into the number of points contracted.

3. Add your result to the interest rate agreed upon.

For example, if you have a 15-year mortgage at 8 percent and are charged 3 points, your effective rate is 8.2 percent. Simply divide the 3 points by 15 years and add the result to the interest charged to find your effective yield:

$$3 \div 15 = .002 \text{ or } 0.2\%$$

$$8\% + 0.2\% = 8.2\%$$

Here is another way to compare mortgage loans. Assume you are offered this choice: a 30-year, $100,000 mortgage with 3 points (costing you $3000 up front) at 7.5 percent ($700 monthly) versus a no-point 8 percent ($734 monthly) mortgage. Which would be more advantageous to you? The difference in your monthly payments would be $34 ($734 − $700). If you took the 7.5 percent loan, the $34 monthly savings would go toward your getting back your $3000 (3 points), and you would break even in less than 8 years. This means that every month after the eighth year, you would be ahead by $34 a month. Over the 30-year mortgage, you could save close to $9000.

If the payment of points is properly executed, it is usually deductible in the year you take out the mortgage. How can you make certain whether you will get the tax deduction? The best method is to ask the lender whether the points are considered a prepayment of interest or a service fee. Prepayment of interest is deductible, while a service fee is not.

If the bank certifies that the points represent a prepayment of interest, to be on the ultra conservative side and ensure your deduction, pay the points with a separate check. Don't allow the bank to deduct the points from the mortgage. Suppose, for instance, you borrow $60,000 and owe 4 points. Don't accept a check from the bank for $57,600 ($60,000 less the $2400 payment of points). Instead, ask for payment of the full mortgage amount, and then hand over your own check for $2400. Note that this does not apply to the refinancing of a home. The tax law states that you can fully deduct points only on a mortgage incurred "in connection with" the purchase of your principal residence. This means that the "all at once" deduction is limited to the mortgage you first take out when you buy your home and not to its refinancing, as with a home equity loan; with refinancing, you must amortize (spread out) the point cost over the life of the loan.

What Is a Home Equity Loan?

Up to this point, we've been concentrating on the most common type of mortgage loan—the "first mortgage"—normally taken out to make home purchase possible. However, many homeowners who already have mortgages are taking advantage of the equity they have built up in their homes by borrowing against that equity. These loans are called *home equity loans* and are a convenient source of needed cash. Many banks will lend up to 80 percent of the equity of your home—that is, the value of your home less the unpaid balance of your mortgage—without requiring lengthy loan applications or long waits for approval. However, do not fall into the trap of thinking that the net value of your home (after mortgage liability is considered) always becomes the amount you will be able to borrow on a home equity loan.

Consider this scenario: You have a $200,000 home with a $75,000 mortgage remaining. The bank states that its limit for a home equity loan is 80 percent of the appraised value. Therefore, you assume that the loan amount will be:

$200,000	Value of home
− 75,000	Mortgage remaining
$125,000	Equity in home
× 80%	Bank's appraisal limit rate
$100,000	Line of credit for home equity loan

Wrong! Because of little home appreciation in the early 1990s, many lenders have become very conservative in their method of computation. In the above example, even if you have $125,000 of equity in your home, you will not be able to receive 80 percent of it. Rather, the lender could compute your line of credit in the following manner:

$200,000	Value of home
× 80%	Bank's appraisal limit rate
$160,000	Bank's appraisal limit
− 75,000	Mortgage remaining
$ 85,000	Line of credit for home equity loan

Also remember that after you take out a home equity loan, you will have to make two monthly loan repayments (one for the original mortgage and one for the second mortgage) to retain your ownership of a single piece of property.

Like first mortgages, home equity loans have varying terms. When the interest rate is fixed, the term is usually 15 years or less; when the interest rate is variable, the term may be up to 20 years or in some cases even longer. The payback period on this second mortgage is usually shorter than on the first mortgage. In addition, you may be charged one or more extra points for a home equity loan, but today many banks are waiving this added cost. Also, although the points are deductible for refinancing on home equity loans, as stated before, they cannot be deducted all at once but must be gradually written off over the years that you remain in the house. On the original purchase of a home, however, you can deduct the cost of the points at one time.

What Tax Ramifications Are There with Home Equity Refinancing?

Immediately after the 1986 Tax Reform Act, U.S. taxpayers found that they had lost most of their interest deductions on personal debt. But by taking out a home equity loan, they were still able to deduct the interest charges regardless of the purpose the funds were used for. The laws have changed slightly, but within the limits of sensible debt management it is still advantageous to secure a home equity loan when you need money. For other than home equity debt, a cap of $100,000 (on top of the loan you took out to purchase the home) is deductible. You cannot use the money, however, for the purchase of tax-exempt bonds.

This type of borrowing is an ideal method for financing a child's education: It is often less expensive than a normal personal loan, the interest you are charged is tax-deductible, and the payback period can be spread over 20 years. Or you may use the funds for needed medical expenses or for just "you" and that dream "retreat" that you were never able to afford. In today's economy, financing for vacation homes is not always readily available, and when it is, it is usually encumbered with stringent restrictions. Now, through home equity loans, these impossible dreams can become a reality.

And on the topic of mortgages, it is amazing that yesterday's nest egg can't buy today's birdhouse.

12

Mortgages— In Reverse

A conventional mortgage will turn your income into equity while a reverse mortgage will turn your equity into income.

In the previous chapter, we discussed the conventional mortgage. Let's reverse the topic. The year 1993 saw interest rates fall drastically. Because of these low yields many older people found it difficult to make ends meet. They own their own home, with a great deal of equity in it, but they do not have sufficient income to live out their remaining years in the lifestyle that they have dreamed about. Most of these people are house rich and cash poor. Certainly they can sell their home for additional cash, but then where would they live? They can borrow through home equity loans (only if they qualify and have sufficient current income which most do not), but they must still pay back a portion of the debt each month. What to do? The reverse mortgage (RM)! Bear in mind that the topic of reverse mortgages can be a lengthy and complicated one. I will attempt in the next few pages to give you a clear, concise overview of what this program is all about, but more research on your part is needed.

What Is a Reverse Mortgage (RM)?

The reverse mortgage is a home loan that is treated in the opposite fashion of a standard mortgage because the money goes from the lender (a bank, for example) to you, the homeowner. In other words, instead of you borrowing a large amount of money and making small monthly repayments back to the lender, you borrow small amounts over a period of year, even for the rest of your life.

You do not give up any ownership when you take out an RM. All privileges of ownership stay with you as well as all responsibilities (taxes, insurance, maintenance, etc.). If you sell your home, the money that is owed becomes due and will come from the proceeds of the sale of the home. If you die before any sale is made, your estate will pay the amount that is owed. In other words, you can live in the house for the rest of your life, receive monthly income during your lifetime, and have your estate pay the debt after your demise. It costs you nothing.

To be eligible for a RM (lenders have different requirements) you must own your home (usually with little or no debt) and you must be of a minimum age. You do not want to be too young (in your early sixties) to take this out, since your monthly income will be much less than if you were 10 years older. The reason that higher monthly income increases for older people is that the number of years that they have left to live will be less, the value of their home will have increased, and the possibility of one of the spouses becoming widowed is greater.

There are many different methods of payments to you.

1. Single lump-sum payment
2. Lifetime monthly advances (most popular)
3. Monthly advances for a specific period of time
4. A line of credit
5. Any combination of the above

What Is the Structure of the Reverse Mortgage?

All reverse mortgages are known as "rising debt" loans because the amount you owe grows larger over a period of time. After you receive your first monthly advance, that is the amount that you will owe. But the next month you will receive more money and that is added to what you already owe from the month before. The pattern goes on for each and every month that you live. You own the home during your lifetime and title rests with you. However, if your heirs fail to repay the loan when the due date arrives (usually upon your death), the lender has the right to foreclose the property. Most RMs allow you to prepay the loan at any time.

Medicare and social security eligibility are not based on either your assets or your income. Therefore, whatever advances you receive from the RM will not affect any benefits you receive from public programs. If you receive SSI, RM monthly advances will not affect your benefits as long as you spend the money within the month you receive it.

Bear in mind, and this is most important, that all income you receive from the RM (whether monthly or in a lump sum) is nontaxable. That means that every penny you get to keep.

Of course, certain disadvantages are attached to the RM. The costs attributed to reverse mortgages (closing fees, points, etc.) are usually higher than the costs of other loans, and the interest rates charged by the lender are on a compounding basis. Also, this type of mortgage will give your heirs less equity in the home you leave them.

How Is the Amount of Payment to You Determined?

The amount of money you receive from your lender will depend upon three factors:

1. *Age:* How old you are at the closing of the mortgage will determine in part the amount of your income. Naturally the older you are, the more money you will receive, since you have fewer years left to receive this income. If you are married, some lenders will use the age of the younger spouse; others will average the two life ages together in order to determine their payment to you.

2. *Equity:* The value of your home will determine the monthly income you will receive. Some lenders may have minimums or maximums on the value of your home.

3. *Costs:* The costs of closing fees, insurance, and interest will determine the net amount of your monthly receipt.

For clarification, there is a big difference between a standard (also known as forward) mortgage and a reverse mortgage. In a standard mortgage, your monthly payments to the lender become equity for you in the future, whereas in a reverse mortgage you turn your present equity into monthly income (as a debt). In other words, a standard mortgage builds up your equity with each payment you make, while a reverse mortgage spends down your equity with each payment you receive.

The two major forms of RMs are the public-sector loans made by state and local governments and the private-sector loans made by mortgage lenders (banks, savings and loans, credit unions). Our discussion focuses on the private sector.

How Does the FHA Reverse Mortgage Work?

Of all private types of RMs (the others being the insured mortgage and the uninsured mortgage), the FHA reverse mortgage appears to be the most popular. Congress passed in 1987, and amended in 1989, housing legislation authorizing 25,000 federally insured reverse mortgages under the Federal Housing Administration (FHA) Department of Housing and Urban Development (HUD). This law will remain in effect until September 1995 and provides RMs with federal insurance that will protect both the lender and the borrower. In order to be eligible for the RM, the borrower must be at least 62 years old and own a single-family dwelling. Condominiums must be FHA approved to be eligible, whereas co-ops, multiple dwellings, and mobile homes do not qualify. You may choose the method of income payment that meets your specific needs.

Three plans are offered:

1. The *tenure plan* provides monthly repayments to you for as long as you live in your home. These payments will continue until you die, sell, or move away.

2. The *term plan* provides a monthly advance for a specific number of months that you select (higher income each month than the tenure plan). When the time period runs out and the lender's repayments to you cease, you are not required to make payments back to the lender as long as you live in the house.

3. The *line of credit* lets you decide when you would like additional cash. If you combine the tenure or term plan with the line-of-credit plan, you will have not just income each month but also the option of meeting any unexpected expenses (having to leave your home for health reasons, for example) that may occur in the future. Remember that your concern is in the future, because that is where you will be spending the rest of your life. Advantages to the FHA-insured RM are many: There is a wide choice of payment options, the loans are backed by the federal government, and no repayment is required until you die or move away. For a list of lenders, write to Home Equity Information Center; AARP Consumer Affairs, 601 E Street NW, Washington DC 20049.

What Other RM Plans Are Offered?

Two other RM plans are available to the general public: the lender-insured reverse mortgage and the uninsured reverse mortgage. The lender-insured plan is based on the concept that lenders will create their own private pool of insurance with FHA help. This plan generally has the same procedures and benefits as the FHA reverse mortgage, but the amount of its advances is usually greater. Under this insured plan, you can request only a percentage of your home equity to go toward the RM, thus reserving part of the value of your home for yourself or your heirs. For example, on a $100,000 equity, you may decide to mortgage only 70 percent ($70,000) and keep the balance ($30,000) for the future. Thus the lender, at payoff time would recover, at most, only the $70,000 that was loaned. Your 30 percent share would always be in your estate. One more point. Lender-insured loans can become very expensive if homes appreciate at a high rate. Yet the overall cost of this type of loan is low if you exceed your life expectancy and the home appreciates at a low rate.

The uninsured reverse mortgage (also known as the fixed-term RM) is structured differently from the other two types mentioned. The loan is paid out to you for a fixed period of time (usually 5 to 10 years) in monthly payments. The length of the loan will have a major impact on the amount of money you receive monthly. A 5-year term, for example, can pay you as much as three times the monthly amount as a 10-year term. This imbalance occurs because you are allocating the same value of your home over a longer period of time, and the longer the term of the loan, the more the effect that compounding interest has on its cost. When the time period ends, no additional income is sent to you. The loan must be repaid at that point. This type of loan is designed only for a person who needs monthly income for a specific period of time and who intends to sell the home at that point. Do not consider this type of RM if your plans are indefinite or if you intend to live in your home forever.

However, the uninsured RM does provide a greater amount of monthly advance than the other two types.

What Other Information Should You Know about the Reverse Mortgage?

Under the HUD agreement, there is a maximum amount that your home can be valued at, and each area (urban versus rural) has different limits, somewhere between $67,500 and $124,875. This limit is known as "203-b-2," but you should not concern yourself if your home is worth more than the maximum. It will not make you ineligible if your value is greater, but it does mean that the amount determined by 203-b-2 will be the highest value placed on your home.

Watch out for the "default" clause that appears in some contracts. This acceleration means that certain conditions could force you to sell your home before you die. These may include extended stay at nursing-care facilities, failure to pay property tax, failure to maintain and insure the property, personal bankruptcy, fraud, and condemnation proceedings.

Remember that a RM is a loan only against your home equity; thus you can never owe more than the value of your home at any time. This limited liability is known as the "non-recourse" limit, stopping the lender from seeking more money from your other assets or from your heirs. In other words, if you should live many years more than was expected (thus receiving more income than your house is worth) the lender cannot go after your estate to make up the difference.

You can look at the RM in the same manner as a single-premium annuity policy. In the annuity concept, you receive a monthly income for the rest of your life by taking money out of your capital and paying one lump-sum payment in advance. The reverse mortgage works in similar fashion but instead of giving the lender a large amount of money, you merely put up your house as the collateral for the funds. The big difference is that you still have your capital.

The lending institution that holds your reverse mortgage

will get the money it paid to you (principal, interest, and costs) when the home is sold. These costs should be examined closely. Although the interest rate that is charged to you is the one that is most visible, expenses can vary considerably and may include origination and insurance fees, interest on loan advances, and of course closing charges. The best way to treat all the various charges involved is to insist that all loan costs be combined into one single rate known as the total annual percentage rate (TAPR) which becomes due at the loan's maturity.

The lender must send you monthly advances until you sell, give away your home, or die. At that time, under any of these conditions, the money owed is paid back to the lender. However, the vast majority of homeowners will never themselves actually pay back the money that has been advanced to them. Rather, it will be paid after their death by their estate, normally from the sale of the house. You can almost say that you will enjoy your money "while you are living" and your heirs will have to meet your obligation when you die, keeping only the remainder for themselves. Remember, you are not taking money out of your childrens' pocket. What you are doing is putting a little less in. In other words, you are spending part of your children's inheritance. What a pleasant thought. And on the topic of children, if you want your children or grandchildren to turn out well, spend twice as much time with them and half as much money on them.

13

Municipal Bonds—
The Tax-Free Choice

You work hard all your life to reach a high tax bracket and then the government goes and lowers it on you.

With the new tax plan of the Clinton administration in 1993 (especially with the higher tax rates), the desire for untaxed income has become stronger than ever. Since tax-exempt bonds yield about 85 percent of comparable taxable instruments, the investor in the 28 to 39.6 percent tax bracket has a chance to lock in excellent returns.

How Do Municipal Bonds Work?

Today, few local or state governments have on hand the vast sums of money needed to build schools, roads, water and sewer facilities, and other public works. Some towns, cities, and counties are finding it difficult even to meet their daily operating expenses. But these social needs won't just disappear. In order to meet these expenses, communities borrow money from citizens and institutions by issuing debt obligations known as municipal bonds (munis). There are over 40,000 different governmental units and agencies currently issuing municipal bonds. They include states, cities, towns, counties, and such agencies as highway departments and housing authorities.

What Types of Bonds Are Available?

Among the more popular varieties of municipal bonds available are the following:

1. *General obligation (GO) bonds:* These are backed by the full faith and credit of the issuing agency. Interest payments on GO bonds are supported by the taxing authority of the state or city government and are generally considered the safest form of municipal bonds.

2. *Revenue bonds:* These are usually issued by a government agency or commission that has been charged with operating a self-supporting project, such as a highway or bridge. The money raised through the sale of revenue bonds goes to finance the project, and the income realized from the completed project (tolls, for example) is used to pay the interest and principal on the bonds. However, if the project should earn insufficient income, bondholders may be left holding the bag; the taxpayers of the community are not responsible. The reason is that if revenue bonds default, the courts are reluctant to auction off the bankrupt assets so that the bonds can be repaid. Municipal assets are viewed as being vital for the public welfare; thus their sale could place the community in jeopardy. Therefore, your risk is greater in buying revenue bonds but your yield is a bit higher.

What Are the Advantages and Disadvantages of Municipal Bonds?

The advantages of municipal bonds are as follows:

1. *Tax exemption:* For the investor, the most important advantage of municipal bonds is the fact that they earn income which is tax-free at the federal level. If you live in the state in which the bonds are issued, the bonds are usually free from state and local taxes as well. However,

Illinois, Wisconsin, Iowa, Oklahoma, and Kansas will tax some in-state bonds.

2. *Safety:* Municipal bonds have historically been a very safe form of investment, since states and cities, with their power of taxation, have normally been able to fully meet their debt obligations.

3. *High collateral value:* It's usually possible to borrow up to 90 percent of the market value of your municipal bonds from such lenders as banks and brokerage houses, since municipal bonds are free of certain restrictions imposed by the Federal Reserve Board on the use of other bonds as collateral.

4. *Diversity:* Thousands of different municipal bonds are available to suit the requirements of individual investors.

5. *Marketability:* A large nationwide market for municipal bonds exists, making them easy to sell when necessary. However, you should never buy municipal bonds for speculation. Purchase them for the tax-free income they produce and only in anticipation of "what you can get from them, not for them."

Attractive as these features may be, municipal bonds are not for everyone.

1. *Investment:* A fairly sizable investment is needed with a minimum investment of $5000 usually required.

2. *Yield:* Tax-exempt municipal bonds usually carry a lower rate of interest than taxable bonds. If the tax rate you pay is fairly high, your tax savings will more than make up for the lower return; but those near the bottom of the tax rate tables may be better off with another investment.

3. *Social security:* Under the new tax law effective in 1994, if you are collecting social security benefits, there may be a problem because, while the interest you receive from these bonds isn't taxable for federal purposes, it may force you to pay federal income tax on up to 85 percent

of your social security benefits. See Chapter 25 on social security for the computation.

Are Municipals Your Best Investment?

To determine whether or not you should invest in municipal bonds, you must figure out the taxable rate of return equivalent to that paid by tax-exempt municipals. For example, suppose you have a marginal income tax rate of 28 percent, and you are offered a tax-exempt municipal bond paying 6 percent interest.

To find the equivalent taxable rate of return: (1) take the difference between your marginal tax rate and 100 percent and (2) divide this into the rate paid by the tax-exempt bond. Since your marginal tax rate is 28 percent, the difference between this and 100 percent is 72 percent. Divide 72 into 6 and you obtain a result of 8.3 percent. Thus, a tax exempt interest rate of 6 percent is equivalent to a taxable interest rate of 8.3 percent for someone in the 28 percent tax bracket.

The formula below will help you determine the equivalent taxable yield (ETY):

$$\frac{\text{Yield on MUNI}}{1.00 - \text{tax bracket}} = \text{equivalent taxable yield (ETY)}$$

$$\frac{6\%}{1.00 - .28} = \frac{6\%}{.72} = 8.3 \text{ ETY}$$

Table 13.1 shows several typical tax-exempt interest rates along with the equivalent taxable yield for investors in various tax brackets. For example, for an investor in the 28 percent tax bracket, a 6 percent tax-exempt yield is equivalent to an 8.3 percent taxable yield.

This taxable-equivalent yield of 8.3 percent means that you would need a taxable instrument paying almost 9 percent to equal your 6 percent tax-exempt bond. By using this table, you

Table 13.1. TAXABLE-EQUIVALENT YIELDS UNDER FEDERAL RATES, 1994

Tax-free yield	15%	28%	31%	36%	39.6%
3.50	4.12	4.86	5.07	5.47	5.79
3.75	4.41	5.21	5.43	5.86	6.21
4.00	4.71	5.56	5.80	6.25	6.62
4.25	5.00	5.90	6.16	6.64	7.04
4.50	5.29	6.25	6.52	7.03	7.45
4.75	5.59	6.60	6.88	7.42	7.86
5.00	5.88	6.94	7.25	7.81	8.28
5.25	6.18	7.29	7.61	8.20	8.69
5.50	6.47	7.64	7.97	8.59	9.11
5.75	6.76	7.99	8.33	8.98	9.52
6.00	7.06	8.33	8.70	9.38	9.93
6.25	7.35	8.68	9.06	9.77	10.35
6.50	7.65	9.03	9.42	10.16	10.76
6.75	7.94	9.37	9.78	10.55	11.18
7.00	8.24	9.72	10.14	10.94	11.59

will be able to determine the type of taxable return you would have to receive to exceed the tax-exempt return from your muni. Also, bear in mind that state tax is not considered in this example, so your yield is actually higher than 8.3%. And on the topic of state tax, Table 13.2 depicts the approximate equivalent yield factor of both federal and state tax using 31 percent, 36 percent, and 39.6 percent federal tax brackets.

To find a taxable-equivalent yield (TEY), multiply the in-state municipal bond yield by the appropriate TEY factor for your state. This will give you the approximate yield needed on a taxable investment to equal the yield on a state and federal tax-free bond. For example, a New York State resident in the 31 percent tax bracket purchasing a New

Table 13.2. TAXABLE-EQUIVALENT YIELD UNDER STATE RATES, 1994

State	31%	36%	39.6%	State	31%	36%	39.6%
AL	1.50	1.64	1.74	MT	1.57	1.75	1.86
AK	1.45	1.56	1.65	NE	1.54	1.67	1.78
AZ	1.54	1.68	1.78	NV	1.45	1.56	1.65
AR	1.56	1.68	1.78	NH	1.53	1.64	1.74
CA	1.63	1.75	1.86	NJ	1.56	1.64	1.78
CO	1.50	1.64	1.74	NM	1.58	1.70	1.81
CT	1.51	1.63	1.73	NYC	1.64	1.76	1.87
DE	1.57	1.69	1.79	NY	1.57	1.69	1.79
DC	1.60	1.72	1.83	NC	1.57	1.69	1.79
FL	1.45	1.56	1.65	ND	1.61	1.77	1.88
GA	1.54	1.66	1.76	OH	1.56	1.68	1.77
HI	1.59	1.73	1.84	OK	1.56	1.68	1.78
ID	1.58	1.70	1.80	OR	1.59	1.71	1.82
IL	1.49	1.61	1.71	PA	1.49	1.61	1.70
IN	1.50	1.61	1.71	RI	1.58	1.70	1.81
IA	1.56	1.73	1.84	SC	1.56	1.68	1.78
KS	1.54	1.67	1.76	SD	1.45	1.56	1.65
KY	1.51	1.66	1.76	TN	1.54	1.66	1.76
LA	1.51	1.66	1.76	TX	1.45	1.56	1.65
ME	1.60	1.73	1.84	UT	1.56	1.68	1.78
MD	1.54	1.67	1.76	VT	1.59	1.71	1.81
MA	1.65	1.77	1.88	VA	1.54	1.65	1.76
MI	1.58	1.70	1.80	WA	1.45	1.56	1.65
MN	1.56	1.70	1.81	WV	1.55	1.67	1.77
MS	1.53	1.64	1.74	WI	1.54	1.67	1.78
MO	1.52	1.66	1.76	WY	1.45	1.56	1.65

York State bond at 6 percent would have to get a taxable yield of 9.42 percent (6 percent × 1.57) to equal the yield on the federal and state tax-free bond.

Are Municipals a Risky Investment?

As with any investment, risk is a factor to consider in purchasing municipal bonds. Like corporate bonds, municipal bonds are rated by two major independent rating services: Moody's and Standard & Poor's. The AAA rating is the highest; the C rating is the lowest. In general, the lower the rating, the higher the yield. However, I don't recommend that you purchase bonds with a rating lower than A, since the slightly higher interest rate you may be offered on the lower-rated bond isn't worth the sacrifice in safety. Also, when financial times are as uncertain as they are today, investors will look for high-quality bonds even though they do produce a lower yield.

One way to virtually eliminate the risk in buying municipal bonds is to buy bonds that carry a third-party guarantee offered by companies such as the Municipal Bond Insurance Association (MBIA), the Financial Guaranty Insurance Company (FGIC), Capital Guaranty (CG), and the American Municipal Bond Assurance Corporation (AMBAC). If the municipality should fail, the insurer will continue to make timely payments of interest and principal as agreed upon at the time of purchase. In addition, the insurance will add to the liquidity of the investment, since potential buyers appreciate the greater safety of the insured bonds.

Here's how it works. When a municipality issues muni bonds, the city's or state's credit is on the line. If bonds are low-rated, the municipality must pay higher-than-normal interest on the issued bonds. To save money, it may purchase insurance which guarantees that all payments of principal and interest will be made on time. It thus may appear that the insurance is free to the investor, but that is not true. Since the insurance raises the quality of the municipality's credit, the yield on the bond issued will be lower. And one more point. The cost/yield difference between an insured and an uninsured bond is so narrow that today the insurance has become a "good buy."

Can Municipal Bonds Be Called Back?

Callability is a significant factor affecting the value of municipal bonds. Bonds that offer higher interest rates than what is presently being offered are most likely to be called in, because the issuer will want to redeem these costly older bonds and replace them with new ones paying lower yields. And this is so true today. When a bond is callable, it may be redeemed by the issuing agency prior to the maturity date, usually within 10 years after issue, and usually at a premium (2 percent) $1020 for each $1000 face value of the bond. Of course, this places a lid on potential profits, which may be a significant loss to you if interest rates decline greatly after the bond is issued.

From the middle of 1993 to 1995, approximately $200 billion in muni bonds will be called back. And of all the investors that this call will affect, "bearer holders" (see page 43) will be the hardest hit. The reason is that these bearer holders may not know that their bonds have been recalled. Because these bonds are not registered in anyone's name, the issuer does not have a record of who owns them. By law, the city or state that issued the bonds to be called, must notify bearer holders by placing notices of the calls in the newspapers. However, if the investor does not read a business newspaper, he or she may miss the call notice and lose several months (up to a half year) of interest. In some cases, the bonds may be sitting in a vault for many years. If that situation should occur, no interest on these bonds would accrue from the date of the call. Thus, you hear that the best bonds today have a "call protection" feature that prohibits the issuer from calling them back. However, try to find them in today's low-interest market.

Are There Strategies in Purchasing Municipal Bonds?

One method of diversifying a bond portfolio is a technique better known as laddering. What is done is that you purchase bonds maturing in different years. Therefore, if rates have risen when a bond matures, you will be able to reinvest the proceeds into an instrument paying the new high yield. Conversely, if interest rates should fall, a portion of your holdings will still earn interest at the higher (earlier) rates.

Also, look into pre-refunded premium bonds. These bonds are issued by states and municipalities in order to reduce the high-double-digit interest costs of bonds issued by them during the early 1980s. What happens is that the issuer will sell, at a lower rate, a second series of bonds maturing on the date when the old bonds can be called in early. The proceeds of the second series are invested in Treasury obligations giving safety to the old issues.

How Do You Find the Best Bond Value?

Get quotes from several brokers before buying bonds. Prices on previously issued bonds vary greatly from dealer to dealer, since each sets his or her own profit margin individually. The difference between what the broker pays for the bond (known as the bid price) and its selling price (known as the asking price) is the "spread." Brokers do not charge commissions on bond trades but make their money on this difference (quoted in basis points which are hundredths of a percentage point). Remember, the longer the maturity and the smaller the trade, the wider the spread. Before buying, ask your broker what he or she would pay to buy the bond back on the following day. This will show any hidden charges such as fees and markups. The matter is further complicated by the fact that municipal bonds are not listed on any exchange, making it that much harder to gauge prices. This caveat doesn't apply to new issues; the issuer pays the dealer's markup on those, so that you'll get the best price no matter where you buy. Therefore, seek out all information before purchasing. And on the topic of information, the jawbone of an ass is just as dangerous today as it was in Samson's time.

14

Municipal Trusts and Funds— Tax-Free Alternatives

A government is the only vessel known to leak from the top.

At one time, tax-free benefits were available only to the well-to-do because any purchase of municipal bonds under $25,000 was considered an "odd-lot" amount and would cost you extra brokerage commissions (as well as being harder to sell later). Under these conditions, the municipal bond market was strictly a high-priced investor's playground, and the cost of establishing a diversified portfolio of many municipal bonds was extraordinarily high. It was to remedy this situation that the municipal bond unit trust and the municipal bond mutual fund were developed.

What Are Municipal Funds and Trusts?

In some ways, the municipal bond unit trust and the municipal bond mutual fund are similar. Both offer a way for the small investor to buy a portion of a diversified selection of municipal bonds for as little as $1000. Both offer investments that are free of federal income taxes and, in some cases, state and local taxes (if you live in the state in which the bonds were issued). Also, both pay interest on a monthly basis, unlike the municipal bonds themselves, which pay interest only semiannually.

However, there are many differences between the unit trust and the mutual fund. Let's explore these differences so that you can decide which of the two might be worth considering as an investment for you.

How Does the Unit Trust Work?

A municipal bond unit trust is established by a sponsor who purchases a substantial share in at least 10, but more often 20 or more, long-term bond issues, usually with maturities ranging from 10 to 30 years. The bonds bought by the trust are left intact and do not change once they have been purchased. Therefore, the yield of the trust remains the same throughout its life span, which has a predetermined length that ends when the bonds in the portfolio mature. When you buy a share in a unit trust, you are buying a portion of this fixed portfolio, and you can predict just how long your investment will last and how much it will pay each year.

There are many types of unit trusts, and they vary greatly in terms of their length of maturity, degree of risk, tax-exempt status, and yield. The chances are excellent that you can find a trust with the right combination of features for your investment needs. You can buy units in a trust either directly, from the sponsoring firm, or indirectly, through your broker. It pays to work through your broker, who can offer you trusts assembled not only by his or her own firm but by other companies as well.

Once all the units in a particular trust have been sold, no more can be issued. You can dispose of your units without incurring a penalty or sales charge by asking your broker or the sponsoring firm to redeem them. In most cases, unit trust sponsors constitute a secondary market for their own units, and will guarantee to buy back your units at their current market value. Of course, this may or may not represent the same amount as you originally paid. If interest rates have risen since the trust was assembled, the rate being paid by the trust may no longer be competitive, and the market value of the units will be less than what you paid for them. On the other hand, if interest rates have fallen, you may make a profit when you sell your shares.

Because the portfolio of a unit trust is basically fixed, "managing" the trust is very simple. Therefore, a very small management fee is normally charged. However, when you purchase units in the trust, you must pay a commission which ranges from 2 to 5.5 percent, depending on the company sponsoring the trust, the length of maturity, and other factors.

What would happen if one of the bonds in the trust should run into financial difficulties? Normally, the trustee may decide to sell that specific issue in the trust; however, unlike fund managers, trust managers are not permitted to add any new issues to a portfolio once it has been created. This tends to make trusts slower to respond when a bond's creditworthiness is in doubt. Also bear in mind the risk of early redemption. Many new issues are callable, meaning that the bonds can be called back after a specified period of time. This may occur if interest rates fall by more than 2 percentage points, so beware of high-yield projections. Every trust prospectus must inform you of which bonds in its portfolio are subject to call and their dates of possible callability.

How Does the Municipal Fund Work?

A municipal bond mutual fund is similar to a money market fund: Its shares are highly liquid. Each fund sells or redeems shares at its net asset value at any time, with some funds permitting redemption by wire transfer and even allowing investors to move from one fund to another by telephone. Whereas a bond unit trust stands pat with its investments, the managers of a bond fund are constantly trading. Thus the fund as a whole never matures but goes on indefinitely buying and selling bonds to take advantage of changes in the marketplace. Because of this continuous activity, a higher management fee, compared with that of the trust, is charged, usually about 0.5 percent annually.

Participation in a bond fund usually requires an initial investment of $1000. Any time thereafter you can buy additional shares in the fund. You have the option of receiving a check for your monthly earnings or having them automatically reinvested to purchase additional shares in the fund. Whenever you wish, you can sell your shares back to the fund. However, since the value of the bonds in the fund's portfolio fluctuates over time, you may or may not get back your original investment when you sell your shares.

How Does Insurance Affect the Trust or Fund?

Insured unit trusts and funds are normally not a good value, since the trust or fund is formed around many individual units, not just one bond. For example, a trust having 15 bonds that saw one of its bonds lose all its money would suffer a loss of only 6.6 percent. Since the cost of insurance over a 10-year period averages about 3 percent, you can see that you pay an extremely large premium to protect yourself from a minor loss. You're gambling on about 100-to-1 odds.

What Are the Basic Differences between the Trust and the Fund?

The differences between the municipal bond unit trust and the municipal bond mutual fund are summarized in Table 14.1.

If you're not sure whether a unit trust is a better investment for you than a mutual fund, follow this rule of thumb:

Table 14.1. THE MUNICIPAL BOND TRUST AND FUND COMPARED		
	Unit trust	Mutual fund
Yield	Fixed	Varies with market conditions
Life of investment	Ends when bonds mature	Unending; constantly changing portfolio
Average maturity of bonds held	10–30 years	3 years or less
Purchase	Fixed number of units offered	Shares always available for purchase
Portfolio	Same bonds (15–20 issues) held to maturity	100 or more bonds actively managed
Disposal	Units sold through brokers, as with stocks	Shares sold back to fund

The unit trust is a better choice if you are certain that you want to hold onto the investment for at least 5 years. If you think you may need to liquidate your holdings sooner than that—or if you anticipate shifting to other investments fairly frequently—the mutual fund is preferable. Either investment, however, is a good way for the small to medium-sized investor to get into municipal bonds with a diversified, professionally selected, tax-free portfolio of holdings.

However, you should be aware of how interest-sensitive municipals are. In times of stable interest rates, their after-tax yields are better than most investments (for the high-tax-bracket investor), and should interest rates decline, they can add capital gains as well. It is when rates move upward that the bonds may become a problem, because capital losses can occur upon their sale.

Another problem that funds and trusts are currently experiencing involves two distinct areas: (1) the questionable quality of the bonds bought by funds and trusts looking to boost their yields, and (2) the threat that bond-rating agencies might lower the grades on many munis because of the ever-growing financial strains that may cripple state and local governments. Therefore, a word of caution. Look toward safety when considering muni funds or trust, staying only with those funds that invest at least 90 percent of their portfolio in A or better rated bonds. You can get this information from the company's annual report, ask the salesperson, or write to the company. Also, bear in mind that the tax-free status of municipals affects retirees with a total modified adjusted gross income greater than $34,000 and couples with an income greater than $44,000, since they must pay taxes on a portion of their social security income. For the purposes of this computation, modified adjusted gross income includes tax-free municipal bond income, thus diminishing the value of the tax-exempt status of municipal bonds, trusts, or funds for retired people.

I have attempted in this and the preceding chapter to explain the concepts of municipal bonds, trusts, and funds. The lower marginal tax rates compared to ten years ago might seem to neutralize the main advantage of such issues. But, remember, this is a double-edged sword. While tax rates have fallen, many of the deductions and shelters have been partially or fully eliminated, therefore leading to increased rather than decreased taxes. Also, if Congress raises income taxes (higher than the present 39.6 percent level) to offset the huge deficit, or it extends limitations on issuers of municipal bonds (in other words, it cuts the supply), the value of present-day municipals will rise greatly. When you compare them with the taxable investment yields in Table 14.2, you can see why the municipals, whether they be in the form of bonds, trusts, or funds, represent a variable financial instrument in the money world today.

And on the topic of taxes, Form 1040, the tax return we all file, could just as easily have been numbered 1039 or 1041. The IRS has assured the American public that the number 1040 was a random selection. Still, some taxpayers insist it's

Table 14.2. TAXABLE INVESTMENT YIELD BEFORE AND AFTER TAX CONSIDERATION	
Taxable investment yield	After federal and state tax deducted*
5.0%	3.0%
5.5	3.3
6.0	3.6
6.5	3.9
7.0	4.2
7.5	4.5
8.0	4.8
8.5	5.1
9.0	5.4
9.5	5.7
10.0	6.0
*Assumed combined tax, 40 %.	

not a mere coincidence that in Coventry, England, Lady Godiva, covered only by her long hair, rode naked through the streets protesting the high, oppressive taxes imposed by her husband, the Earl of Coventry, in the year 1040.

15
Mutual Funds—
Spreading the Risk

If you risk nothing, you risk everything.

Since October 1987, we have experienced stock market plunges and record-breaking rises that today are still causing anxiety among investors. If you still feel uncertain about the market but would like to take some active part, a mutual fund may be ideal. Look at the growth trends. In 1990, mutual fund assets were estimated at $1 trillion. By the end of 1993, this figure had doubled to over $2 trillion.

How Does the Mutual Fund Work?

A large number of investors put their money together in a pool to be managed by knowledgeable investment professionals. The price of a share in the mutual fund is determined by the value of the fund's holdings. As the value of the stocks owned by the fund increases, the share price increases and the investors make a profit; if the value of the stocks decreases, the shares are worth less and investors suffer a loss. The price of a share in a mutual fund (determined by dividing the net value of the fund's assets by the number of shares outstanding) is usually announced once or twice a day. The mutual fund also earns dividends that may be paid directly to investors or reinvested to buy additional shares in the fund.

Therefore, mutual funds can make money for their investors in three distinct ways:

1. The shareholders receive dividends earned through the investment that the fund possesses.

2. If a security in the fund's portfolio is sold at a profit, a capital gains distribution will be made by the fund to its shareholders.

3. If the value of the fund's portfolio increases, the value of each share also increases.

Mutual funds are normally created and managed by brokerage houses. As you'll learn, there are many kinds of mutual funds, depending on the types of stocks invested in, the degree of risk involved, the financial goals of the fund, and other factors. There's a definite advantage to investing in a fund which is part of a "family of funds." This is a group of mutual funds with differing investment objectives managed by the same company that allows you to move your money from one fund to another (by written notification or by telephone), thus offering you maximum flexibility with a minimum of paperwork and lost time.

A way to take care of market fluctuations in the mutual fund arena is through dollar cost averaging (DCA). The investor puts into the mutual fund the same amount of money at regular intervals (monthly, for example). This system allows the investor to purchase more shares when prices are low and fewer shares when prices are high. Although this method can work with any investment, it works particularly well with mutual funds because funds have a diversified portfolio and can bounce back quickly from declines. Table 15.1 presents an example. For the investments shown, the average price of a share was $11.25. But the investor using the dollar cost averaging method paid only $8.89 on average. This means that the average cost per share was $2.36 less than the average price.

One more point on market fluctuations, many funds

Table 15.1. HOW DOLLAR COST AVERAGING PAYS OFF			
Month	Regular investment	Share price	Shares acquired
January	$200	$10	20
February	200	5	40
March	200	10	20
April	200	20	10
TOTAL	$800	$45	90

Average share cost: $8.89 ($800/90)
Average share price: $11.25 ($45/4)

advertise how high their total return was for a period of time. If you are more interested in knowing the average annual rate of gain rather than the total return, which is the compounded average annual rate, examine Table 15.2.

What Are the Advantages of Mutual Fund Ownership?

Mutual funds offer eight important benefits to prospective stock market investors:

1. *Diversification and risk control:* Money invested in a mutual fund is used to buy shares in many different stock issues. This reduces your investment risk, since the failure of one or two companies out of many will not have a devastating effect on your portfolio. It would be impossible for an individual investor to achieve a comparable degree of diversification without having a very large sum to invest in a variety of stocks. Also, with a small investment amount, you will find that by "doing it yourself" your transaction costs (commissions) will be very high because you will be transacting in small dollar amounts. Remember that diversification takes both time

Table 15.2. AVERAGE ANNUAL RATES OF RETURN		
Total return		Average annual rate
3 Years	5 Years	
15.76%	27.63%	5%
19.10	33.82	6
22.50	40.26	7
25.97	46.93	8
29.50	53.86	9
33.10	61.05	10
36.76	68.51	11
40.49	76.23	12
44.29	84.24	13
48.15	92.54	14
52.09	101.14	15
56.09	110.03	16
60.16	119.24	17
64.30	128.78	18
68.52	138.64	19
72.80	148.83	20

and a great deal of knowledge. And one more point: in the prospectus, the terms *diversified* or *nondiversified* may be used. A diversified fund must have at least 75 percent of its total portfolio in different securities so that no one investment can make up more than 5 percent of the fund's total assets. In a nondiversified fund, the requirement is reduced from 75 to 50 percent. However, as important as diversification is, the concept that stock funds shield you from stock market plunges is not always true. Even though there is a good amount of diversification (many different stocks in the same fund), if the market should tumble (as in 1987 and 1989) or fluctuate (as in the huge market swings in the early 1990s), diluting the risk by spreading your portfolio among many different stocks does nothing when virtually every issue falls.

2. *Professional management:* Few investors have the time, energy, or expertise to keep track of all the many factors affecting the stock market, including changes in interest rates and the money supply, new developments in technology, legal and political developments, and foreign competition. Mutual fund companies have the resources to monitor these developments, for they employ staffs of researchers whose sole task is to keep track of business and economic trends that may affect the performance of securities in the fund's portfolio. This expertise works to your benefit when you invest in the fund.

3. *Moderate cost:* Many mutual funds require only a small initial investment, with management fees averaging 0.5 percent of your investment annually. By buying or selling in large blocks, the mutual fund pays a brokerage commission that is but a fraction of what you, the small investor, might have to pay. Also, certain types of securities should be bought only in large amounts. For example, Treasury bonds produce the best prices on trades of $1 million or higher—far more than most of us can afford—but such trades are no problem for the mutual fund. For more information, see the discussion of load and no-load funds in the section on costs later in this chapter.

4. *Fund-swapping option:* Many investment firms sponsor more than one type of mutual fund. The firms usually allow their investors to move money from one fund to another by means of letter or phone call. This is a convenient way to take advantage of changing investment conditions.

5. *Automatic deposits:* You can usually arrange for automatic investments to be made in your mutual fund account by specifying a dollar amount to be withdrawn from your bank account on a regular basis. This provides a painless

way of building your investment portfolio month by month.

6. *Automatic reinvestment:* You can have all dividends, interest, and capital gains earned by your investment automatically reinvested in additional shares in the fund, another painless way of keeping your investment growing. *Warning:* Some funds may charge a fee of up to 7 percent for reinvesting dividends. Make certain that your monthly statement says that the offer is at "net asset value" and not that the reinvestment of the dividend was at the "offering price."

7. *Ease of withdrawal:* You can usually withdraw your funds by means of a letter authorizing the redemption of shares. You'll normally receive your money within 7 days.

8. *Reduction of record keeping:* The fund handles all stock transactions for you, records any changes in your holdings, and provides periodic statements showing all transactions, dividend distributions, reinvestments, and capital gains. However, always keep a detailed record of how many shares you buy, the date of each purchase and the cost per share. This also includes any dividend reinvestment. It is important because if you do not identify the specific shares you are selling, the rule of "first in, first out" applies, meaning that the basis of the shares you are turning in will be considered to be the ones that you own for the longest period of time. This will have a major drawback, since the early shares are often the lowest priced. Thus your taxable profit will be higher.

What Are the Different Types of Mutual Funds?

Depending on your financial circumstances and your investment objectives, there are many types of mutual funds from which to choose. Let's consider the features of the most common types of funds.

Common-Stock Funds

Many funds invest in common stocks issued by corporations. Stock funds are often classified as either growth funds (holding riskier stocks that may pay low or no dividends but are expected to rise in value rapidly) or income funds (holding low-risk stocks that pay higher dividends but rise in value slowly). Different types include:

- *Aggressive growth:* Small-company growth funds, sector funds, precious metals funds, and others that seek maximum capital appreciation

- *Long-term growth:* Funds whose main objective is long-term growth of capital; income is secondary

- *Global/international:* Funds that invest worldwide, outside the United States only, and single-country funds

Investing in stock mutual funds may be riskier than investing in Treasury bills or bonds, but do you get anything out of these government investments? Look at the figures. During the past 68 years, inflation averaged more than 3.2 percent while Treasuries returned an average of less than 3.8 percent (bills) and 5.2 percent (bonds)—hardly keeping up with inflation, much less making any money. By contrast, over that same period, common stocks returned more than 12.5 percent with small company stocks averaging 17.6 percent.

Bond Funds

Bond funds invest in corporate or government bonds. These funds fall into several categories. High-grade bond funds deal in top-rated bonds with a high degree of safety and modest yields. Speculative bond funds deal in somewhat riskier bonds (with ratings in the high B's) that often pay higher yields. Junk-bond funds carry both the greatest degree of risk and the greatest potential yield. But recently they have come under great pressure because of the losses they have incurred. And municipal bond funds invest in tax-free bonds issued by state and local governments.

In order to choose a mutual fund that is best for you, consider these factors:

1. *Past performance:* It is more likely that a fund with a good performance record will repeat its good record than that a company with a poor performance will turn itself around.

2. *Expenses:* The less a fund takes out of your payments (management fees, commissions, etc.), the better off you will be since more money is being invested on your behalf.

3. *Risk:* Risk comes in two forms. The first type of risk is the possibility that rising interest rates will bring down the value of the bond. As you are aware, higher interest rates have a direct reverse effect on fixed-rate securities such as bonds. Thus, short-term bond funds are less risky than intermediate- or long-term bond funds. The second area of risk involves credit risk—the risk that the issuer of the bonds will not pay. Funds that invest in government securities are thus considered very safe.

    Warning: The name of Uncle Sam in the title of a mutual fund is a great advantage. However, what most people do not know is that a fund calling itself "Government Securities Fund" has to invest only 65 percent of its assets in that single security. Thus "Government Securities Fund" can still invest 35 percent of its assets in something that is not government insured. That is the reason some funds are able to pay high yields. A portion of their portfolio may be in junk (high-yielding but risky) obligations.

4. *Management:* Good management is of course essential for profit. Look at the portfolio turnover of your fund. This will tell you how often a manager sells the instruments in the fund and buys new ones. Remember that the more the selling and buying, the more commissions that have to be paid. Also to be considered with respect to high portfolio turnover is that the manager may be buying

instruments, not on their merits, but rather in anticipation of short swings in the market. This is a situation that is risky and may not work in the long run.

5. *Your goals:* What is the reason for the creation of your fund? Did you buy it for your child's education? For retirement? The goal you set up will determine the type of mutual fund you will want to purchase. Thus a time horizon is very important for your financial decision making. You may need the money in 10 years for your child's education but in 25 years for your retirement. For a long period, up-front load is not as important as a large annual maintenance charge.

As your investment needs change over time, so do the types of funds which are best for you. When you are young, growth funds are usually best. Your financial needs are often modest at this time, and you can afford to take on a higher degree of risk in exchange for maximum growth potential. As you and your family grow older, diversification among various types of funds is desirable. Both stock funds and bond funds belong in your portfolio in middle age. For maximum diversity, try a five-prong approach: domestic and international stock and bond funds and money market funds. This has the effect of offering you three types of financial instruments—stocks, bonds, and cash—both in the United States and in foreign countries. When you are getting near retirement age, current income becomes paramount. Bond funds are probably your best choice at this point. And investors of any age who find themselves in a high tax bracket should consider one of the tax-free funds which invest in municipal bonds or other tax-free investments.

What Are the Costs of Owning a Mutual Fund?

Depending on how they are purchased, mutual funds can be classified as either load or no-load funds. Let's look at the difference.

There are people who use self-service gas pumps and there are those who prefer service; the same goes for mutual funds. If you are not certain as to your current income needs, your risk involvement, and/or the price fluctuations of market investments, or if you simply don't have the time to be "involved," then the load fund is for you.

Shares in a *load fund* are sold through a stockbroker, who charges a sales commission that normally is about 6 percent of the purchase price (this is the *front load*). This commission—about three-quarters of which is kept by your individual broker while the balance goes to the sponsor of the fund—is deducted from your account before any investment is made. If you deposit $10,000 in a mutual fund that charges a load of 6 percent, only $9400 will actually be invested in the fund. Depending on the performance of the fund, it could take several months to a year or more for you to recoup the $600 commission. However, if you plan to remain in the fund for a number of years, the initial sales charge will become relatively unimportant over time. An annual management fee of about 0.5 percent of your investment is usually also charged.

What does your commission fee pay for? Primarily you are paying for the advice and services provided by your broker. As an investment professional, he or she should help you select the best fund or funds for your purposes and should keep you continually informed as to when you should move in or out of a particular instrument. If your broker doesn't provide this kind of expert advice, consider changing brokers; after all, you're paying for it.

No-load funds are usually sold through the mail by means of advertisements in newspapers or magazines. No sales broker is involved; therefore, no up-front commission must be paid. However, a service charge is levied each year. Also, you may have to pay an exit or redemption fee (rear-end load) when you withdraw from the fund. No sales advice or investment services are offered with a no-load fund.

No-load funds do not charge commission fees, because their shares are bought directly from the funds and not through the brokers. Recently, however, some funds have been imposing sales and distribution charges without the investor noticing them. These new "no-load funds" have what are called distribution fees which cover the cost of commissions in the same manner as front loads. Also, some of these funds have redemption fees that you will be charged if you redeem your holdings within the first few years, starting around 6 percent and declining to zero in about 6 years.

Are you aware that the no-load funds are allowed to have these fees because of a little-known regulation? In 1980 The Securities and Exchange Commission (SEC) added rule 12b-1 to the Investment Company Act, permitting mutual funds to charge shareholders for the cost of getting more assets into the fund. In other words, a fund could charge the investor for advertising, sales literature, and brokers' commissions on new fund sales. Fund managers felt that they were justified in charging these fees since in the long run, fundholders would benefit as operating costs were spread over more assets. Thus expense ratios would go down and all would benefit. What is considered an equitable expense ratio? A rule of thumb might be that no more than 1 percent annually for stocks and 0.75 percent annually for bonds should be charged. In 1993, caps were placed on these charges.

In the past, funds could hide these 12b-1 costs by scattering them throughout the entire prospectus (a booklet containing information to help evaluate the investment being offered), thereby hiding the fund's true cost. In 1989 the SEC enacted new rules that required funds to disclose all fees and expenses in one table near the front of the prospectus. This table must show all expenses (both direct and indirect) paid by shareholders, and must also disclose the cumulative expenses paid on a $100 investment (5 percent return assumed at the end of 1-, 3-, 5-, and 10-year periods). In order to understand more about the instrument, remember the following poem, which I came upon years ago:

> Before you invest always read the prospectus.
> It's required by laws designed to protect us.
> Buried somewhere under mountains of prose
> Are all the risks to which you're exposed.
> So to understand the data, let me give you a hint.
> The greater the hazard, the smaller the print.

Today these 12b-1 charges bring in well over $1 billion in additional fees to the ever-growing mutual fund business.

One more point on the prospectus. As of this writing, the SEC has made suggestions concerning mutual funds that may shortly be enacted into law. I am concerned about these proposals, which may hurt the middle-income investor. One of the most blatant proposals is to allow the consumer to purchase mutual funds by "coupon clipping." Let me explain. Presently, mutual fund companies can only advertise their product and send you information (known as a prospectus) about their management, fees, investment philosophy, risks, and so on. They are not permitted to sell you the investment directly until you receive all this information. Now the SEC is proposing to abolish the prospectus ruling and allow people to clip the coupon in the advertisement and send in their check so that they can immediately purchase the fund. This method of purchasing a fund from an advertisement is called buying "off the page" and appears to be a deregulation of mutual fund marketing. Please ask for the information before purchasing any investment, no matter how good those advertisements look. Coupon clipping could become a dangerous situation for the unsophisticated investor.

How Do You Compute Your Taxes on Mutual Funds?

The computation of payment of taxes on earnings from a mutual fund can be a very complicated affair. Always keep a detailed record of the amount of shares purchased and the date and price of each share. Include in this figure any shares you bought through a DRIP (*d*ividend *re*investment *p*rogram). Remember that the income earned each year on your mutual fund shares is taxable as it is earned regardless of whether you take it out in cash or reinvest in additional shares. When you sell your shares, you will have either a capital gain or loss which is based on the difference between your tax basis (what you paid plus charges) and what you received from the sale. There are three methods to determine your cost when you have purchased shares over a period of years at different prices.

1. You can identify specific shares that you wish to sell in writing to your broker and these will form the basis of your cost.

2. If no instructions are given other than to sell, the first-in, first-out method will apply.

3. If you wish, you may use the average basis of all your shares in the fund.

What Information Is Available?

Each newspaper that carries daily information about the value of mutual funds may list data in different ways. Figure 15.1 is a standard reading of mutual funds as listed in the financial section of your newspaper.

The NAV (net asset value) states what each fund is worth. The figure is computed by totaling the market value of all the fund's assets and adding one day's interest and dividends received. The result is then subtracted by one day's expenses and administrative fees. The total is divided by the number of shares outstanding resulting in the amount for the NAV. Understanding these figures is important.

Let's look at an example. Yields reported on the same funds may produce different amounts. The yield in an advertisement you read is called the SEC yield because it is based on a strict conservative formula devised by the SEC and can be the only rate used for advertising. The problem with this yield is that the figure suggests income you would

NAME	NAV	BUY	CHANGE
Joy Fund p	12.38	13.15	+.04
Happy Fund r	6.48	6.96	− .03
Smiley Fund t	18.86	19.09	− .12
Glad Fund	11.64	N.L.	+.19

Explanations

NAV (bid): Net asset value per share (in dollars and cents).

BUY (ask): Price paid by investors plus commission.

CHANGE: Change in NAV from yesterday

Symbols

p: Fund imposes a 12b-1 charge.

r: Fund imposes a back-end fee (redemption price).

t: Used when both p and r are applied

N.L.: Signifies no front- or back-end load.

Figure 15.1. Sample mutual fund listing.

earn if you were in the fund for a full year and the fund kept paying at its current rate, which may not always be the case. However, some publications may cite the 12-month average yield, which represents all the fund's income pay-out per share for the past year divided by the NAV. This method expresses what the fund actually paid into fund-holders over the past 12 months. Thus, think of yields and NAV as opposite sides of a seesaw. The interest income is in the middle and stays the same as long as the fund's hold-ings do not change. As the NAV goes up, the yield goes down. As the NAV goes down, the fund's yield from that same amount of income goes up.

And on the topic of information and advice, I have noticed that when a person with money meets a person with experience, the person with the experience gets the money and the person with the money gets the experience.

16

Real Estate as Security and Investment

A lot of homeowners have discovered that trees grow on money.

The real estate market has certainly cooled down since its fantastic rise in the preceding decade. However, regardless of economic conditions, there are certain basic concepts that should be understood.

What Are the Benefits of Real Estate?

When you buy real estate for use as rental property, you can benefit by the purchase in at least three ways: It provides current income; it provides tax benefits through business expense deductions and depreciation; and, if you like, it can provide a place to live when you retire.

Let's consider first the tax benefits which result from offering property you own for rental purposes. First, any expenses you incur in operating the rental property are deductible from your income as business expenses. These might include repair and maintenance of the house or other property, interest payments on a mortgage, or an occasional trip to inspect the property if it is outside your own residential area.

144

Second, depreciation can be deducted from your income as well. This is the annual decline in value of any property which results from its increasing age. Depreciation is determined according to a fixed schedule depending on the nature of the property; a house, for example, is usually assumed to have a depreciable life of 27.5 years, so that you can deduct from your income a specified percentage of the house each year over a 27.5-year period. This is a noncash deduction, since you are not actually expending any money; yet you reap tax benefits just as if you were. Also, until 1993, real estate losses could be applied only against real estate gains because they were considered to be passive. However under the Clinton tax change, passive real estate losses can be deducted from nonpassive income if you spend more than 50 percent of your time in a real-estate-related business such as construction, development, rental management, leasing, or real estate brokerage.

Interestingly, real estate values usually increase each year rather than decrease, despite what happens in "soft" markets such as in the early 1990s. Therefore, you could say that you benefit twice: The actual resale value of your real property will generally grow, while you get a tax deduction because of the theoretical decrease in the value of your property over time.

Real estate, then, offers decided advantages to the canny investor. But like any other investment, it carries risks as well. The greatest is the risk of buying a property whose rental or resale value is minimal. It has been said that the three most important rules of real estate investment are location, location, and location, and that advice is pretty sound. There's no substitute for knowing the property and its actual value well. Never buy property you haven't personally visited and inspected. Photos or videotapes shown by an agent are no substitute; you'll never see the drawbacks of the property in that way. There are plenty of places in the world where no one is living and where no one will ever want to live. If you buy one of them, your chance of renting or selling the property is small, and mortgage payments, taxes, and other expenses will still have to be met. So above all, make sure you know the property before you buy.

What Rules Govern Investing in Real Estate?

1. Never buy property solely for its depreciation value. If a piece of real estate isn't a good investment in its own right, its tax benefits will not make it worthwhile.

2. Don't buy commercial property if you're a beginner in real estate investing. Single homes and small apartment houses are safer investments and more reliable sources of income.

3. Buy property within your own community, where you know property values and can anticipate trends. Your chance of success in the real estate field decreases as the distance from your home base increases.

4. Use as little cash as possible when buying real estate for investment purposes. Make a small down payment and take out the largest fixed-rate mortgage you can afford.

5. Don't invest in real estate unless you can reasonably foresee an annual profit from your investment (after deducting expenses and taxes) of at least 15 percent. The property itself should have a reasonable prospect for appreciation of about 10 percent annually.

6. Remember that renting can mean headaches for you as a landlord. The property must be maintained according to health and safety standards set by local governments, and complaints from tenants can be annoying. You might consider having a professional manager operate your property, but his or her fee, ranging from 6 to 10 percent of the rent, will cut heavily into your profit.

What Are the Tax Benefits of Selling a Home?

Another important aspect of real estate investments is the selling of your home and its tax ramifications. When you sell your home and a profit is realized, you will get two favorable tax treatments:

1. You will be able to postpone the tax on the profit indefinitely if you purchase another primary residence within 2 years.

2. Under certain conditions, you may take a one-time capital gains exclusion of $125,000 against the profit from the sale of the home. This exclusion can include untaxed profits on previous homes so long as the total does not exceed the $125,000 limit. You will qualify for this exclusion if:

   - You are 55 or older.
   - You own and have occupied the home as your primary residence for at least 3 of the last 5 years before the sale. This 3-year occupancy rule may be accumulated with temporary absences during the 5-year period. Even if you rent, as long as it is not more than 2 years (during the 5-year period), the renting will not hurt your ability to use the $125,000 exclusion.
   - Neither you nor your spouse has ever taken this exclusion before. If your spouse has already taken the exclusion, even if it was prior to your marriage, neither of you can claim another exclusion unless the original exclusion was revoked within 3 years. Within 2 years of selling your home, if you purchase and live in another home that costs at least as much as the adjusted sale price of the old home, your entire gain on the sale is not taxed. In that case, you should save your $125,000 exclusion and use it when you sell your second home. But if you sell your home and purchase another home for an amount *less* than the home you sold, you might be better off taking the $125,000 exclusion now.

Is There an Alternative to a Direct Real Estate Purchase?

If you're interested in real estate investment but somewhat hesitant to get involved directly, consider a real estate investment trust (REIT). It is the simplest and most direct way to invest in real estate. Like a mutual fund, a REIT pools money from many investors who buy shares in the trust's portfolio. However, rather than investing in stocks or bonds, a REIT invests in real estate.

Purchasing a REIT could be looked at as investing your money in real estate by the share instead of by the brick. When you receive shares in a trust, you are buying a stock that trades on a stock exchange just as any other stock does. Income from rent or interest on the mortgages are paid as dividends to the shareholders. These securities are required by law to pass through 95 percent of the income they generate to shareholders in the form of dividends. When the property is sold, capital gains will be given to the stockholders as a special dividend; or the sale may increase the earnings per share, thus raising the value of the stock. REIT investments fall into two basic categories:

1. *Equity:* This type of trust should be chosen if you feel that there will be higher inflation. Remember that the higher the inflation, the greater the chance that your property values will increase and rents will rise.

2. *Mortgage:* If you feel that inflation will remain low, then the mortgage REITs' yields will look very attractive against a background of stable or even falling interest rates. All REITs, like bonds, rise in value when interest rates fall as investors run to higher-yielding securities. But because they are highly leveraged, these mortgage REITs will react much more intensely to interest rate movements than the equity REITs. For example, when rates fell sharply following the bloated years of 1980 to 1981 (15.75 percent in 1981 to 11.5 percent in 1982), mortgage REITs climbed an average of 44.6 percent compared with the equity REITs' 20.4 percent gain.

REITs have a number of advantages for investors. They allow small investors to participate in real estate investments that would otherwise be unavailable. Shares in a REIT are liquid and can normally be sold at or near their full value. They are a liquid method of owning what is traditionally an illiquid asset. REITs are easier to buy and sell than physical property. There are over 100 REIT funds traded on the New York and American stock exchanges and the NASDAQ national market system.

As long as a REIT meets certain requirements, it pays no corporate tax. Thus, while other investments, such as mutual funds, pay after-tax dividends, the REIT can distribute pretax dollars. One additional point. Under the old law, pension funds were not permitted to invest in REITs. However, in 1993 this ban was lifted.

Naturally, REITs have their disadvantages. Management and operating fees reduce the net earnings of the trust and the amount of investor distributions as well. The tax benefits normally associated with real estate ownership—including deductions for depreciation, interest, and maintenance costs—are absorbed by the trust rather than passed on to individual investors. REITs normally do not have to pay taxes. However, you, the investor, do, since most dividends received from these trusts are taxable at regular rates. There is an exception. Dividends paid out to shareholders' equity (which represents a return of capital) are not taxable. Also, remember that any loss occurring from your REIT can be used to offset capital gains you made during the year. Any loss over gain can be deducted from your income for up to $3000 annually. And one last point: REITs do not always get the best real estate choices, since many of the smaller REITs have trouble competing for properties with real estate syndicates, insurance companies, and large pension funds.

Financier J. P. Morgan once said, "The time to buy straw hats is in the winter." This concept also applies to real estate assets today. As history has shown, timing is most important, and the best time to buy is when an asset is not in total favor with the investing public. The REIT is a good example.

REIT investments may be very conservative or highly speculative, depending upon the policy set by the management of the trust. You'll want to make sure that the objectives of the trust match your own investment plans before you get involved. Here are some points you should be aware of when considering REITs.

1. Depreciation charges have changed. Previously, the law permitted you to group deductions into a 19-year period and take the largest ones in the early years. The Tax Reform Act (TRA) has now extended the time period of 27.5 years for residential and 31.5 years for commercial property bought after December 31, 1986. To add to this, the depreciation must be taken steadily over the years instead of at an accelerated rate.

2. Any profit received from the sale of real estate will be more heavily taxed because of the elimination of long-term capital gains. Prior to 1987, 60 percent of the profit on property held for more than 6 months was tax-free. It no longer is.

3. Be careful about selecting trusts that use large amounts of short-term debt to finance long-term mortgages. If short-term rates go up, your holdings could face serious trouble.

4. The total management fees and other charges should not exceed 1 percent of gross assets a year. Try to choose a REIT that is "self-administered," meaning that the managers are employed by the trust.

5. Avoid newly formed REITs. As far as I am concerned, the trust should have a track record of at least 3 years. Also, look for a dividend growth of at least 10 percent annually.

Over the past 3 decades, real estate values in the United States have soared, with few other investments showing such a comparable growth. If the U.S. economy continues to prosper, real estate will continue to benefit. As long as you know what you're buying, the chances are that you can do very well by investing in real estate. And on the topic of real estate, by the time you finish paying for a house in the country, it's no longer the country.

17

Stock Market—Bulls, Bears, and Pigs

In the bust of 1987, I made a killing in the market. I shot my broker.

Just prior to October 19, 1987, everyone was witnessing a major surge in the stock market. Money was being made everywhere and the golden bubble of prosperity just grew and grew. Then came the inevitable burst in 1987 and again in 1989. It is said that bulls can make money and bears can make money, but pigs get slaughtered. And that is exactly what happened.

There's no doubt that investing in the stock market can be one of the most exciting ways of making money. Nothing quite compares with the thrill of seeing the little-known stock you picked become a hot property, perhaps doubling in price—and then doubling again and again. But as with any investment, the potential risks are equal to the rewards. Middle-income investors who want to play the market owe it to themselves to become fully informed before getting involved. This chapter should be only the beginning of a continuing process of education for anyone interested in becoming a successful stock market investor.

How Does the Stock Market Work?

A share of stock represents a unit of ownership in a corporation. When you buy stock, you are becoming a part-owner of the business. Therefore, you benefit from any increase in the value of the corporation, and you suffer when the corporation performs badly. You're also entitled to share in the profits earned by the corporation.

Stocks are bought and sold in marketplaces known as *stock exchanges*. The exchange itself does not buy or sell stock, nor does it set the price of stock; the exchange is simply a forum in which individuals and institutions may trade in stocks. Stock exchanges play a vital role in a capitalist economy. They provide a way for individuals to purchase shares in thousands of businesses, and they provide businesses with an important source of capital for expansion, growth, research, and development.

There are two types of stock exchanges: organized and unorganized.

There are some 14 organized stock exchanges currently operating in the United States. The New York stock Exchange (NYSE) is both the best known and the largest (over 1300 members). Only members may trade shares on a stock exchange, and only individuals may become members, although a member may be a partner or an officer in a brokerage firm (known as a *member firm*). To become a member, you must buy a membership, or "seat," from another member or from an estate. The price of a seat varies greatly, depending on the volume of business being transacted. Within the last 20 years, a seat on the NYSE has sold for as little as $35,000 (in 1977) to over $1 million in 1987.

Most brokerage firms own seats on an exchange, with one of the firm's officers designated as a member. In their role as brokers, members carry out clients' orders to buy or sell certificates on the floor of the exchange. In communication with other exchange members, brokers can carry out buy-and-sell transactions right on the exchange floor. Current sale prices on each stock being traded are constantly updated and made available to all members. Thus the exchange operates as a kind of auction market for the trading of securities.

How Does an Investor Purchase Stock?

Here's what happens when an investor decides to buy or sell a particular stock.

First, an account executive at the brokerage house receives the buy or sell order, which may take any of several forms:

Round-lot order: An order to buy or sell 100 shares, considered the standard trading unit

Odd-lot order: An order to buy or sell fewer than 100 shares

Market order: An order to buy or sell at the best available price

Limit order: An order to buy or sell at a specified price

Stop order: An order designed to protect profits or limit losses by calling for sale of stock when its price falls to a specified level

Good till canceled (GTC) order: An order that remains open until it is executed or canceled by the investor.

Second, after the order is received, it is sent by teletype to the floor of the stock exchange. The brokerage firm's floor broker receives the order and executes it at the appropriate trading post. Confirmation of the transaction is teletyped back to the account executive at the local office, who notifies the investor. Remarkably, the entire process may take as little as 2 or 3 minutes.

Not all stocks are traded on any of the 14 organized exchanges. Those that are not are traded "over the counter" in the so-called unorganized exchange. Not a physical place, the unorganized exchange consists of thousands of brokers and dealers who trade in about 50,000 different unlisted stocks through telephone or telegraph communication. A computer system, known as the National Association of Securities Dealers Automated Quotations (NASDAQ), is used to provide instant bid and asked prices on stocks.

In the over-the-counter market, transactions are negotiated privately rather than on an auction basis. An investor wishing to purchase a particular unlisted security consults a broker, who contacts other brokers dealing in that stock. The broker offering the stock for sale at the lowest price receives the offer.

Prices of over-the-counter stocks are quoted as both bid and asked prices. The bid price is the final price offered by a buyer, while the asked price is the final price requested by a seller. Trades are normally made when the bid and asked prices approach one another.

What Kinds of Stocks Are Available?

There are two kinds of stocks: common and preferred.

What Is Common Stock and What Investment Strategies Are Associated with It?

Each year, hundreds of new issues of stock, known as initial public offerings (IPOs), are sold to the publics. Although human life ends at the hands of the *undertaker*, it begins for common stock at the hands of the *underwriter*, who sells the stock, at a fixed price, to a group of initial buyers who in turn "farm out" the investment until it reaches the "street"—which is you, the investor.

A share of common stock represents a unit of ownership, or equity, in the issuing corporation. Each share of common stock usually has a par value, which is a more or less arbitrary value established in the corporation's charter and which bears little relation to the stock's actual market value. The market value is influenced by many factors, including the corporation's potential earning power, its financial condition, its earnings record, its record for paying dividends, and general business conditions.

Ownership of a share of common stock carries certain privileges:

1. *A share in earnings:* Each year, the board of directors of the corporation meets to determine the amount of the corporation's earnings that will be distributed to stockholders. This distribution, known as the *dividend,* will vary depending on the company's current profitability. It may be omitted altogether if the company is earning no current profits or if the board elects to plow back profits into growth.

2. *A share in control:* Holders of common stock have the right to vote on matters of corporate policy on the basis of one vote per share held. However, the small investor with only a few shares of stock has little or no practical influence on corporate decisions.

3. *A claim on assets:* In the event of the company's liquidation, holders of common stock have the right to share in the firm's assets after all debts and prior claims have been satisfied.

There are four main categories of common stock, each of which is best for a particular investment strategy and purpose.

1. *Blue-chip stocks:* High-grade, or blue-chip, stocks are issued by well-established corporations with many years of proven success, earnings growth, and consistent dividend payments. Blue-chip stocks tend to be relatively high priced and offer a relatively low-income yield. They are a very safe investment. However, is that your most important concern? Remember, a ship in the harbor is safe, but is that what ships are built for?

2. *Income stocks:* Income stocks pay a higher-than-average return on investment. They are generally issued by firms

in stable businesses which have no need to reinvest a large percentage of profits each year.

3. *Growth stocks:*   Issued by firms expected to grow rapidly during the years to come, growth stocks have a current income that is often low, since the company plows back most of its earnings into research and expansion. However, the value of the stock may rise quickly if the company performs up to expectations.

4. *Speculative stocks:*   Speculative stocks are backed by no proven corporate track record or lengthy dividend history. Stocks issued by little-known companies or newly formed corporations, high-flying "glamour" stocks issued by companies in new business areas, and low-priced "penny stocks" may all be considered speculative stocks. As with any speculative investment, there is a possibility of tremendous profit—but a substantial risk of losing all as well.

What Are the Differences between Preferred and Common Stock?

Preferred stock, like common stock, represents ownership of a share in a corporation. However, holders of preferred stock have a prior claim on the company's earnings as compared with holders of common stock; hence the name *preferred stock*. Similarly, holders of preferred stock have a prior claim on the company's assets in the event of a liquidation, but they have no voting privileges.

Preferred stock also has certain distinctive features related to dividend payments. A fixed, prespecified annual dividend is usually paid for each share of preferred stock. This fixed dividend may be expressed in dollars (for example, $10 per share) or as a percentage of the stock's par value. It must be paid before dividends are issued to holders of common stock.

However, preferred-stock dividends are not considered a debt of the corporation—unlike, for example, the interest due on corporate bonds—because the firm is not obligated to meet its dividend payments. If the corporation is losing money, the board of directors may decide to withhold the dividend payment for a given year. To protect stockholders against undue losses, most preferred stock is issued with a cumulative feature. If a dividend is not paid on cumulative preferred stock, the amount is carried over to the following period, and both dividends must be paid before holders of common stock can receive any dividend. Also, a few companies may offer adjustable-rate preferred stock (ARPS). These issues have cash dividends that will change every 3 months in accordance with the current market interest rates. This type of stock is designed to be more competitive with bonds and thus to make the dividend rate on preferred stock reflect current market conditions.

Some preferred stocks are convertible. This means that shares of preferred stock can be exchanged for shares of common stock issued by the same company. Prices of convertible preferred stocks tend to vary more than those of other preferred stocks, since they are affected by changes in the prices of the corresponding common stocks. Bonds, too, may have a convertibility feature. Convertible corporate bonds can be changed for a fixed amount of shares of common stock. They act like both bonds and stocks. If a company's stock should rise, the convertible bond will go up almost as much because the bond can, at the option of the investor, be changed into higher-priced stocks. If the stock goes down, a convertible bond's fixed yield will still offer the same income as before the drop.

What Are the Advantages and Disadvantages of Stocks?

Like any investment, stocks have distinct advantages and disadvantages. Some of these should have already become apparent. Let's take a systematic look at them. First, the advantages of investing in stocks:

Growth potential: When a company has the potential for growth in value and earnings, so does its stock. If you pick the right stock or group of stocks, you can profit significantly and relatively quickly. History shows that, as a whole, the stock market has had an upward trend in values, with years of gain outnumbering those of decline by better than 3 to 1.

Liquidity: Stocks traded on the major exchanges can be bought and sold quickly and easily at prices readily ascertained.

Possible tax benefits: Growth stocks, which pay low or no dividends so that company profits can be reinvested, provide an effective tax shelter for your profits. As the corporation's value grows, so does the value of your stock, which is a form of tax-deferred income, since no taxes need be paid on these gains until you sell the stock.

When you sell stock, you will make either a profit or a loss. A short-term capital gain (1 year or less) is taxed at your current income tax rate (maximum 39.6 percent from President Clinton's tax package), while the maximum tax on a long-term capital gain is 28 percent. If you have a net capital loss, you can claim up to $3000 per year to offset regular income. Any excess of the $3000 capital loss can be carried forward to succeeding years. However, if you sell shares of stock and take a loss and within 30 days purchase the same stock, you will not be allowed to claim the loss for tax purposes.

Now, the disadvantages:

Risk: There can be no guarantee that you will make money investing in stocks. Companies may fail, stock prices may drop, and you may lose your investment. Remember the saying of one concerned investor, "I am not so concerned with the return *on* my investment as I am with the return *of* my investment."

Brokerage commissions: Most investors need the help and advice of a stockbroker when they become involved in the market. However, high brokers' commissions can largely erode your profits. Since one fee is charged when you buy your stocks and another when you sell them, you are, in effect, forced to pay twice. If you're an unusually well-informed investor, consider one of the growing firms of discount brokers, which provide little or no investment counseling but charge greatly reduced commissions when trading your stocks.

Complexity: The stock market is a complicated subject, and the amount of knowledge needed to be consistently successful is tremendous. Investors who lack the patience, time, or skill to inform themselves about the market often buy and sell on impulse, thereby minimizing their profits and maximizing their losses. If you get into the stock market, be prepared to devote the time and work necessary to make intelligent decisions instead of haphazard ones.

And on the topic of stocks, what keeps most people out of the stock market is the supermarket.

18

Stock Market Information— Where to Get It

*It's not the bulls and the bears on Wall Street
that make you lose money, it's the bum steers.*

Now that you know the basic characteristics of the different kinds of stocks, let's take a look at some of the things you should know to get started in stock market investing. People will spend 5 to 10 hours in comparison shopping for a television that costs $300 but will put $5000 into a stock after a 5-minute phone call from a broker. The next time you want to buy a stock, spend time learning about the market and its offerings. Pretend you are shopping for a TV.

How Do You Learn about Investing in the Stock Market?

An investor's most important tool is information: information about stock prices, movement in the market, and likely business trends. Without plenty of sound information, investment decisions are pure guesswork. The first place to look for information about any stock is the financial pages of your newspaper, and the best place to start is with the columns listing the current stock prices on one or more of the major organized exchanges. Figures 18.1 and 18.2 provide explanations of the information you'll find in those columns and what it means for you as a prospective investor. The sample in Figure 18.1 shows a typical listing for a stock traded on one of the major exchanges.

Newspapers can list only a small fraction of the thousands of stocks traded over the counter. Therefore, a phone call to your broker is a must if you are interested in the day's activity in a particular over-the-counter (OTC) stock.

Newspaper listings for OTC stocks are simpler than those for stocks traded on a major exchange (see Figure 18.2). A newspaper listing is a useful place to start in getting information and analyzing the value of a particular stock. However, it's only a starting place. Facts derived from a corporation's annual report, newspaper and magazine articles about the business, stock market newsletters and columnists' comments, and the advice of your broker can all be helpful. An old saying is very appropriate: "Buy on rumor, sell on news." Hearsay aside, facts are your most important asset.

What Statistics Should You Know to Evaluate Stocks?

Certain statistics that are widely available for any listed stock can tell you a good deal about its investment prospects.

1. *Earnings per share:* The current earnings-per-share figure is one basic measure of the success of a corporation. It is computed by taking the corporation's net profit after taxes, subtracting any preferred-stock dividends, and dividing the remainder by the number of outstanding shares of common stock. For example, suppose XYZ Corporation earned a net profit of $4,300,000 last year, paid a dividend on preferred stock of $300,000, and has 800,000 outstanding shares of common stock. The earnings per share for XYZ Corporation are $5:

High	Low	Stock	Div	P/E	100s	High	Low	Last	Change
(1)	(1)	(2)	(3)	(4)	(5)	(6)	(6)	(7)	(8)
44	16	XYZ	2.50	9	33	$35\frac{1}{4}$	34	35	$+\frac{1}{2}$

(1) High and Low: These are the highest and lowest prices paid for the stock during the previous year (over 52 weeks). This entry shows that the highest price paid for XYZ stock during the previous year was $44 per share; the lowest price, $16 per share.

(2) Stock: Stocks are listed alphabetically by an abbreviated form of the corporate name.

(3) Dividend: The rate of annual dividend is shown; it is generally an estimate based on the previous quarterly or semiannual payment. This entry shows that XYZ is paying an annual dividend of $2.50 per share, or about 7% (2.50 ÷ 35).

(4) Price/Earnings Ratio: This is the ratio of the market price of the stock to the annual earnings of the company per share of stock. As you'll learn later, this is an important indicator of corporate success and investor confidence.

(5) Shares Traded: This is the number of shares sold for the day, expressed in hundreds. In the example shown, 3300 shares of XYZ stock were traded. The figure does not include odd-lot sales. Note: if the number in this column is preceded by a "z," it signifies the actual number of shares traded, not hundreds.

(6) High and Low: These are the highest and lowest prices paid for XYZ stock during the trading session (that is, the business day). The highest price paid for XYZ stock was $35.25 per share; the lowest price, $34 per share. Stock prices are shown in dollars and fractions of dollars, ranging from $\frac{1}{8}$ to $\frac{7}{8}$.

(7) Closing Price: The final price of XYZ stock for the day. In this case, it was $35 per share.

(8) Change: The difference between the closing price of the stock for this session and the closing price for the previous session. Since XYZ stock closed at $35 per share, up $\frac{1}{2}$ (or 50 cents) from the previous close, yesterday's closing price would have been $34.50.

Figure 18.1. Sample stock listing.

Stock	Bid	Asked	Bid Change
PENY	$7\frac{1}{4}$	$8\frac{1}{4}$	$+\frac{3}{4}$

Stock: The abbreviated name of the issuing company.

Bid: This is the price at which dealers are willing to buy the stock—in this case, $7.25 per share.

Asked: This is the price at which dealers are willing to sell the stock; it is always higher than the bid price. In this case, it is $8.25 per share.

Bid Change: This is the difference between the bid price today and the bid price at the close of the previous day. Since today's bid price is up $\frac{3}{4}$ from the previous day's close, the bid price yesterday was $6.50 per share.

Figure 18.2. Sample OTC stock listing.

$4,300,000	Net profit after taxes
− 300,000	Dividend on preferred stock
$4,000,000	
÷ 800,000	Outstanding shares of common stock
= $5	Earnings per share

2. *Book value:* This is one measure of the value of the assets of the corporation. It is computed by taking the listed value of the assets, subtracting amounts due to creditors and preferred stockholders, and dividing the remainder by the number of outstanding shares of common stock. To take another simple example, suppose XYZ Corporation owns assets valued at $30 million, has debts totaling $10 million, and has 800,000 shares of common stock outstanding. The book value of XYZ Corporation is $25 per share:

$30,000,000	Assets
− 10,000,000	Debts and value of preferred stock
$20,000,000	
÷ 800,000	Outstanding shares of common stock
= $25	Book value per share

3. *Price/earnings (P/E) ratio:*   This important index allows you to compare the market price of the stock to its demonstrated earning power. A low P/E ratio—say, under 7—shows that the company has high earnings relative to the current market price of its stock and suggests that the market has undervalued the stock. The stock is probably a good buy at its current price. Stocks with low price/earnings ratios can reward you in two ways:

   ▪ If they're undervalued, their prices should eventually go up.
   ▪ If the market as a whole slumps, they may not sink as much.

   For cautious investors, stocks with a low P/E ratio make sense. A host of different studies have shown that, as a group, such stocks perform better, over the years, than a group with medium or high P/E ratios. Conversely, a high P/E ratio (15 or more) shows that the market expects large future gains from the company and has therefore driven up the price of the stock. The P/E ratio is computed by dividing the stock's market price by the company's earnings per share. If stock in GUK Corporation is selling at $35 per share and the company has earnings of $3 per share, the P/E ratio is 35 ÷ 3, or 11.6, which is a bit lower than the average P/E ratio of 13.

4. *Yield:*   This figure offers another indication as to how reasonable the current price of a stock is. It is a percentage determined by dividing the current annual dividend per share by the current market price of a share. If XYZ Corporation is paying an annual dividend of $2.50 per share and the stock is selling at $35 per share, then the yield is 2.50 ÷ 35, or about 7.1 percent.

5. *Rate of return:*   The rate of return on a given stock is a measure of the total profit you gain from holding that stock for a specified period of time. Computing the rate of return involves several steps. First, find the total market value of your stock at the end of the period in question. Add to this figure the total amount of dividends

earned by the stock during the period. Divide this sum by the total market value of the stock at the start of the period. Subtract 1, and multiply by 100. The resulting figure, expressed as a percentage, is your rate of return for the period. Here's an example. Suppose you bought 100 shares of AJL stock at $24 per share. You've held the stock for 1 year. The stock paid a $2 per share dividend during the course of the year. At the end of the year, it has a market value of $25 per share. The rate of return for this stock is 12.5 percent, calculated in this way:

$2500	Market value of stock at end of period
+ 200	Dividend paid during period
$2700	
÷ 2400	Market value of stock at start of period
1.125	

$$1.125 - 1.0 = 0.125 \times 100 = 12.5\% \text{ rate of return}$$

Each of these five indicators—earnings per share, book value, price/earnings ratio, yield, and rate of return—is an important factor in judging the value of a stock offering.

What Are Stock Market Indicators?

It has been said that the stock market is a "leading" indicator, meaning that stock prices reflect expectations of future growth and profits. The market is not designed to show current conditions. Thus indexes can yield an idea of what investors are expecting. Most market indexes will move in tandem, but there is a considerable difference in their performances in the long run. The reason is that the indexes are composed of different stocks. Below is a listing of three of the most widely accepted stock market indexes and the types of stocks they include.

1. *Dow Jones Industrial Average (DJIA):*   In attempts to gauge or predict large-scale trends in stock market val-

ues, the Dow Jones Industrial Average (DJIA) is often cited. The most frequently mentioned of four Dow Jones averages (covering industrial stocks, transportation stocks, utility stocks, and a composite average), the DJIA is a barometer of stock market trends based on prices of 30 large U.S. corporations listed on the NYSE. Every day, the fluctuations in the prices of these stocks are combined by adding up the prices of the 30 stocks and dividing the result by a designated factor (used to compensate for complicating situations, such as stock splits and periodic substitutions in the list of stocks used). The 30 stocks that made up the DJIA during 1993 are:

Alcoa	(AA)	IBM	(IBM)
Allied Signal	(ALD)	International Paper	(IP)
American Express	(AXP)	J. P. Morgan	(JPM)
AT&T	(T)	McDonald's	(MCD)
Bethlehem Steel	(BS)	Merck	(MRK)
Boeing	(BA)	Minnesota Mining	(MMM)
Caterpillar	(CAT)	Philip Morris	(MO)
Chevron	(CHV)	Procter & Gamble	(PG)
Coca-Cola	(KO)	Sears, Roebuck	(S)
Du Pont	(DD)	Texaco	(TX)
Eastman Kodak	(EK)	Union Carbide	(UK)
Exxon	(XON)	United Technologies	(UTX)
General Electric	(GE)	Walt Disney	(DIS)
General Motors	(GM)	Westinghouse	(WX)
Goodyear	(GT)	F. W. Woolworth	(Z)

The DJIA has been widely criticized as an inaccurate reflection of the U.S. economy and U.S. stock market. The Dow is weighted with older, heavy manufacturing firms and doesn't fully measure the impact of newer, high-tech companies. The mathematical method used in calculating the Dow has also been attacked on various technical grounds. Other indexes, such as the Standard & Poor's Composite Index (see below), have been created to compete with the Dow. Nonetheless, the Dow Jones Industrial Average remains the most popular and influential measurement of the direction and strength of the U.S. stock market.

2. *Standard & Poor's Composite Index:*   This index, better known as the S&P 500, began in 1957 and is presently one of the 12 leading economic indicators. Although the DJIA is much older than the S&P, many investors believe that the S&P better measures the performance of blue-chip stocks because of its broad base of 500 stocks (compared with the DJIA's 30). These 500 stocks, which are traded on the New York and American stock exchanges and on the over-the-counter (OTC) market, are in turn broken up into subindexes (400 industrial, 40 public utilities, 40 financial companies, and 20 transportation companies) so that a broad base is accomplished. Unlike the DJIA, which measures the returns of a small sector of the stock market (large blue-chip stocks), the S&P 500 measures the performance of many relatively smaller stocks as well as the blue chips. Whereas the DJIA simply adds up the current day's prices of its 30 stocks in its index and begins its calculations from that total, the S&P is weighted by market value (number of shares multiplied by price). Thus each stock can influence the result in proportion to its market value. Another point is that the DJIA moves more dramatically than the S&P 500. In a broad market move, the S&P usually moves 1 point for every 7 points lost or gained by the DJIA.

3. *NASDAQ Composite:*   This index, begun in 1971 by the National Association of Securities Dealers, has risen almost six times its beginning index point. It traces 3900 stocks traded on NASDAQ (formally, the National Association of Securities Dealers Automated Quotations). Like the S&P 500, the index is market-weighted so that

the largest stocks will influence the index more than the smaller ones. Did you know that the 50 largest companies listed on this index have capitalizations of over $1 billion each?

In summary, the past few years since the turbulent changes of the late 1980s have certainly put us on the road to recovery. Even the Persian Gulf War did not play havoc with the market, for new safeguards were in place. It is true that there is no way to tell where the market will be a year or two from now, but by keeping informed, you stand a better chance in this roller coaster market we are now all experiencing. And on the topic of the market, Wall Street is a place where the day begins with good buys.

19

Treasuries Are a Treasure

Everybody wants to eat at the government's
table but nobody wants to do the dishes.

The U.S. Treasury Department has one of the biggest jobs imaginable—providing money for the enormous financial needs of the federal government. No wonder the laws that are created are called "bills." Much of the money the Treasury raises comes from the sale of securities to the general public and institutional investors at an astounding value of $1.7 trillion. These securities are known as *Treasury obligations* and consist of Treasury bills, notes, and bonds.

In a low-interest economy, many people switch to other investments, getting away from their traditional certificates of deposits. If you want a short-term investment, safe and secure, look at the alternative to the CD, the Treasury bill and its longer-term brother and sister, the Treasury note and bond.

What Is the Best Method of Purchasing Treasury Obligations?

Treasury obligations are tax-exempt at the state and local levels and are backed by "the full faith and credit" of the United States. The credit risk involved in this form of investment is considered practically nil (despite what you may have heard about 12-digit federal deficits). In comparison with similar obligations issued by corporations, Treasury obligations usually pay a yield which is 1 or 2 percentage points lower. However, many people are willing to accept the slightly lower yield in exchange for absolute safety. As the saying goes, you can eat well or sleep well, but you can't do both.

Treasury obligations can be bought by direct purchase, at a fee, either through commercial banks or through brokerage houses. However, here is a warning. Although these securities are absolutely safe, to get the guarantee of the U.S. government, they must be registered in your name. If you purchase them from a bank or a brokerage house, you are not covered by the government's guarantee because they may not be in your name. However, the bank or brokerage firm will be covered, since the assurance reverts to the registered owner. That may not be a problem as long as financial conditions are sound, but if your bank or brokerage firm should develop financial difficulty, you may have a problem in securing your money. Therefore, have your name on the instrument as registered to you if you purchase Treasuries from banks or firms. The best way to purchase Treasury obligations is directly from the government (without a fee) through any of its 12 Federal Reserve banks or their various branches.

You may buy Treasury securities in person or by mail, by submitting a competitive or a noncompetitive bid. These bids are called "tenders." Most competitive bids are made by institutional investors, such as commercial banks and brokers, purchasing large amounts of securities. Competitive bidders must specify the percentage yield they are seeking to two decimal places (3.81 percent, for example). When a competitive bid is made, there is the risk of bidding too high and not getting an allotment of the security, since the Treasury usually will accept the lowest bids.

Virtually all individuals submit noncompetitive tenders, which do not require that a yield be specified. These individuals agree to accept the average yield and equivalent price determined by the accepted competitive tenders. Since the treasury usually accepts all noncompetitive tenders, these bidders do not risk rejection of their bid.

There is no limit on the amount you may purchase in any one name by competitive tender. However, noncompetitive tenders in any one name are limited to $1,000,000 for bills and $5,000,000 for notes and bonds.

Tenders must be submitted before 12 p.m. on the auction day. Auctions are not open to observers. Auction results are announced by the Treasury in the late afternoon of the auction day. This information can be found in the financial section of newspapers the next day. Shortly after they are announced by the Treasury, auction results are also available on the Federal Reserve's 24-hour recorded message. A complete listing of Federal Reserve banks is given in Figure 19.1.

Treasury securities are issued in book-entry form only. Under the Treasury Direct System, you establish an account master record when you submit your first tender form. You may review your account master record at any Federal Reserve Bank or branch, or request that a statement of account be mailed to you. It consists of name, address, phone number, Treasury Direct account number, tax information, and payment instructions. It also provides detailed information on all your Treasury securities maintained in the Treasury Direct System. Whenever a change is made to the account information, you will receive a copy of the updated record.

Whenever you purchase a new Treasury security, a statement of account is sent to you listing the description and price associated with each security, and the amount and date of the next interest payment. The statement of account simplifies your record keeping and offers flexibility, since changes can be made quickly.

The Treasury Direct System uses the direct-deposit payment method, whereby interest, discount, and principal payments are electronically deposited into your account at the financial institution you designate. Direct deposit reduces the risk of late payments resulting from lost or stolen checks, ensures that scheduled interest or principal payments will be made to the designated financial institution on the payment date, and allows your funds to earn interest from the payment date if the bank account is interest- bearing.

ATLANTA Securities Service Dept., 104 Marietta St., N.W., Atlanta, GA 30303; (404) 521-8653

BALTIMORE Box 1378, Baltimore, MD 21203 (502 S. Sharp St.); (410) 576-3300

BIRMINGHAM Box 830447, Birmingham, AL 36283 (1801 Fifth Ave., North Birmingham); (205) 731-8708

BOSTON Box 2076, Boston, MA 02106 (600 Atlantic Ave.); (617) 973-3810

BUFFALO Box 961, Buffalo, NY 14240 (160 Delaware Ave.); (716) 849-5000

CHARLOTTE Box 30248, Charlotte, NC 28230 (530 E. Trade St.); (704) 358-2100

CHICAGO Box 834, Chicago, IL 60690 (230 S. LaSalle St.); (312) 322-5369

CINCINNATI Box 999, Cincinnati, OH 45201 (150 E. Fourth St.); (513) 721-4787

CLEVELAND Box 6387, Cleveland, OH 44101 (1455 E. Sixth St.); (216) 579-2490

DALLAS Securities Dept., Station K, Dallas TX 75222 (2200 N. Pearl St.); (214) 922-6770

DENVER Box 5228, Terminal Annex, Denver, CO 80217 (1020 16th St.); (303) 573-2473

DETROIT Box 1059, Detroit, MI 48231 (160 W. Fort St.); (313)-964-6157

EL PASO Box 100, El Paso, TX 79999 (301 E. Main St.); (915) 544-4730

HOUSTON Box 2578, Houston, TX 77252 (1701 San Jacinto St.); (713) 659-4433

JACKSONVILLE Box 2499, Jacksonville, FL 32231 (800 W. Water ST.); (904) 632-1190

KANSAS CITY Box 440, Kansas City, MO 64198 (925 Grand Ave.); (816) 881-2409

LITTLE ROCK Box 1261, Little Rock, AR 72203 (325 W. Capital Ave.); (501) 324-8272

LOS ANGELES Box 2077, Terminal Annex, Los Angeles, CA 90051 (950 S. Grand Ave.); (213)-624-7398

LOUISVILLE Box 32710, Louisville, KY 40232 (410 S. Fifth St.); (502) 568-9236

MEMPHIS Box 407, Memphis, TN 38101 (200 N. Mid-America Mall); (901) 523-7171

MIAMI Box 520847, Miami, FL 33152 (9100 N.W. 36th St.); (305) 471-6497

MINNEAPOLIS 250 Marquette Ave., Minneapolis, MN 55480; (612) 340-2075

NASHVILLE 301 Eighth Ave. North, Nashville, TN 37203; (615) 251-7100

NEW ORLEANS Box 61630, New Orleans, LA 70161 (525 St. Charles Ave.); (504) 593-3200

Figure 19.1. The Federal Reserve system.

NEW YORK Federal Reserve, P.O. Station, New York, NY 10045 (33 Liberty St.); (212) 720-6619

OKLAHOMA CITY Box 25129, Oklahoma City, OK 73125 (226 Dean A. McGee Ave.); (405) 270-8652

OMAHA 2201 Farnam St., Omaha, NE 68102; (402) 221-5633

PHILADELPHIA Box 90, Philadelphia, PA 19105 (100 N. Sixth St.); (215) 574-6680

PITTSBURGH Box 867, Pittsburgh, PA 15230 (717 Grant St.); (412) 261-7802

PORTLAND Box 3436, Portland, OR 97208 (915 S.W. Stark St.); (503) 221-5932

RICHMOND Box 27622, Richmond, VA 23261 (701 E. Byrd St.); (804) 697-8372

SALT LAKE CITY Box 30780, Salt Lake City, UT 84130 (120 S. State St.); (801) 322-7900

SAN ANTONIO Box 1471, San Antonio, TX 78295 (126 E. Nueva St.); (210) 978-1303

SAN FRANCISCO Box 7702, San Francisco, CA 94120 (101 Market St.); (415) 974-2330

SEATTLE Securities Services Dept., Box 3567, Terminal Annex, Seattle, WA 98124 (1015 Second Ave.); (206) 343-3605

ST. LOUIS Box 14915, St. Louis, MO 63178 (411 Locust St.); (314) 444-8703

WASHINGTON, DC U.S. Treasury Division of Consumer Services 20239-0001 (202) 874-4000.

Figure 19.1. (*Continued*) **The Federal Reserve system.**

When you buy a Treasury obligation, you can have its ownership registered in any of four ways:

Single owner: For example, Tom Green (social security number 100-10-1000).

Two owners: For example, Tom Green (100-10-1000) and Betty Green (200-20-2000).

Joint tenancy: For example, Tom Green (100-10-1000) or Betty Green (200-20-2000).

Guardian or custodian for a minor: For example, Betty

Green, guardian (or custodian) for Tom Green, Jr. (300-30-3000).

Treasury obligations can't be registered solely in the name of a minor.

Another method of purchase is to go to the secondary market and buy Treasury issues just as you would any stock or bond. However, this secondary market method does have a hidden transaction cost based on the bid/ask differential (known as the *spread*), to which a retail markup may also be added.

If you purchase through this method, you must keep posted on the market value of the Treasury issue. Newspapers carry the Treasury price quotation each day. Figure 19.2 is an example of part of a one-day's price closing table for U.S. government obligations. The Maturity column shows the maturity date of the issue ("n" depicts Treasury notes). Treasury bond, note, and bill quotes are as of midafternoon. Colons in bid-and-asked quotes represent thirty-seconds. For example 102:03 means $102\frac{3}{32}$. Treasury bill quotes are in hundredths, quoted on terms of a rate of discount. The "bid" price is the highest price (stated as a percentage of face value) that a buyer is willing to pay. The "asked" price is the lowest price that a seller is willing to accept. The Change column shows the amount of price change from the previous day's closing price to the current day's closing price. The Yield column shows the yield to maturity that the investor would earn if the Treasury were purchased at the current market price and held to the maturity date.

What Are Treasury Bills and How Do They Work?

Treasury bills, also known as T-bills, are issued with maturities of 3, 6, and 12 months and are sold in minimum amounts of $10,000 and additional multiples of $1000. They are sold at discount (interest becomes yours immediately) and redeemed, upon maturity, at face value.

TREASURY BILLS

Maturity	Days to Mat.	Bid	Asked	Chg.	Ask Yld.
May 19 '94	65	3.35	3.33	...	3.40
May 26 '94	72	3.41	3.39	+ 0.01	3.46
Jun 02 '94	79	3.49	3.47	...	3.55
Jun 09 '94	86	3.49	3.47	...	3.55
Jun 16 '94	93	3.51	3.49	− 0.02	3.57
Jun 23 '94	100	3.50	3.48	+ 0.01	3.56
Jun 30 '94	107	3.49	3.47	...	3.55
July 07 '94	114	3.57	3.55	+ 0.01	3.64
July 14 '94	121	3.62	3.60	+ 0.03	3.69
July 21 '94	128	3.64	3.62	+ 0.02	3.72
July 28 '94	135	3.66	3.64	+ 0.02	3.74
Aug 04 '94	142	3.70	3.68	+ 0.01	3.79
Aug 11 '94	149	3.71	3.69	+ 0.01	3.80
Aug 18 '94	156	3.74	3.72	+ 0.01	3.83
Aug 25 '94	163	3.75	3.73	+ 0.01	3.85
Sep 01 '94	170	3.76	3.74	+ 0.01	3.86
Sep 08 '94	177	3.78	3.76	+ 0.01	3.88
Sep 22 '94	191	3.78	3.76	...	3.89
Oct 20 '94	219	3.87	3.85	+ 0.01	3.98
Nov 17 '94	247	3.94	3.92	...	4.06
Dec 15 '94	275	3.96	3.94	− 0.01	4.09
Jan 12 '95	303	4.02	4.00	...	4.16
Feb 09 '95	331	4.05	4.03	− 0.01	4.20
Mar 09 '95	359	4.09	4.07	− 0.02	4.26

GOVT. BONDS & NOTES

Rate	Maturity Mo/Yr	Bid	Asked	Chg.	Ask Yld.
8½	Jun 94n	101:12	101:14	− 2	3.52
8	Jul 94n	101:12	101:14	− 2	3.63
4¼	Jul 94n	100:04	100:06	− 1	3.73
6⅞	Aug 94n	101:07	101:09	− 2	3.78
8⅝	Aug 94n	101:30	102:00	− 1	3.79
8¾	Aug 94	102:01	102:03	...	3.69
12⅝	Aug 94n	103:19	103:21	− 3	3.80
4¼	Aug 94n	100:04	100:06	...	3.83
4	Sep 94n	100:00	100:02	...	3.88
8½	Sep 94n	102:13	102:15	...	3.87
9½	Oct 94n	103:02	103:04	− 1	4.05
4¼	Oct 94n	100:02	100:04	− 1	4.05
6	Nov 94n	101:06	101:08	+ 1	4.09
8¼	Nov 94n	102:21	102:23	...	4.09
10⅛	Nov 94	103:28	103:30	...	4.10
11⅝	Nov 94n	104:27	104:29	− 1	4.12
4⅝	Nov 94n	100:09	100:11	...	4.13
4⅝	Dec 94n	100:09	100:11	+ 1	4.18
7⅞	Dec 94n	102:19	102:21	...	4.20
8⅝	Jan 95n	103:15	103:17	− 1	4.29
4¼	Jan 95n	99:30	100:00	...	4.25
3	Feb 95	98:28	99:28	+ 1	3.14
5½	Feb 95n	101:00	101:02	+ 1	4.31
7¾	Feb 95n	103:00	103:02	...	4.33
10½	Feb 95	105:16	105:18	...	4.29

Figure 19.2. Price closing table for U.S. government obligations.

T-bills are sold at auction on a regular basis. It is at this auction that the interest rate to be paid is set, normally resulting from the competitive bids of large institutional investors. Auctions for 3- and 6-month bills are held every Monday, while auctions for 12- month bills are held once a month on any Thursday the government decides.

If you buy your T-bill from a commercial bank or broker, you'll be charged a small fee (which is tax-deductible). If you buy your T-bill directly from the Federal Reserve, no fee is charged. Here's how to go about it:

Bring your payment for a T-bill in the denomination you prefer to a branch of the Federal Reserve bank, making certain that it is received prior to 12 p.m. Eastern Standard Time on the day of the auction. The payment must be by cash, a certified personal check, a bank check, or a matured U.S. Treasury note or bond, and it must be for the full face value of the T-bill. When the auction takes place, the interest rate for the bills sold that day is set, and the amount of the discount to which you are entitled is determined accordingly. You are then sent a check (within 4 banking days of purchase) for the amount of the discount. If no Federal Reserve bank is nearby, you can send for an application by writing either to the Bureau of the public Debt, Division of Customer Services, or to your local Federal Reserve bank. Request the booklet "Basic Information on Treasury Securities— Treasury Direct." If you do not have an application, you can send a letter with a certified check and the following information:

1. Your name, address, social security number, and day-time phone number

2. A statement saying that your bill is noncompetitive

3. The amount (face value) you wish to purchase

4. The maturity of the bill (3, 6, or 12 months)

5. Your account number at your bank (for direct deposit)

Remember, though, that you will lose the opportunity to earn interest during the period from the auction to the settlement date. If you buy your Treasury bill from a commercial bank, although there is a fee of about $50, you continue to earn interest on your money right up to the settlement date because the bank will not transfer your funds until that date.

Do You Receive a Certificate When You Purchase a T-Bill?

The sale of Treasury bills is recorded in book-entry form, meaning that you will not be sent a certificate. The securities are held through the Federal Reserve records in a Treasury Direct account that will be opened when you purchase the securities. Thereafter, all future Treasury transactions will be entered in that account when an order is placed on the tender form. By this book-entry method, you can reinvest the maturing Treasury principal automatically for up to 2 years (eight times for a 3-month bill, four times for a 6-month bill, and twice for a 1-year bill) before you need a renewal request (Form PD4633-2). However, this reinvestment process is treated differently from a mutual fund reinvestment, in which all dividends, interest, and capital gains are invested in more fund shares. The Treasury reinvestment will involve only your original investment. Also remember that you must complete a W-9 (request for a taxpayer identification number). Otherwise, a portion of your proceeds will be withheld to be used for payment of income tax on your earnings.

When the maturity date of the T-bill arrives, you can redeem the bill for its full face value. And since you received the interest (in the form of the discount) in advance, the yield is actually higher than the nominal interest rate.

How Is Interest Paid and What Are the Tax Consequences?

Suppose you buy a $10,000, 1-year T-bill with an interest rate set by auction at 5 percent. After paying your $10,000, you'll receive by mail (see the discussion of Treasury Direct) a check for the 5 percent discount, or $500. Thus the effective price of the T-bill is just $9500. Since you've now received $500 income on that $9500 investment, your true yield is 5.3 percent. To summarize:

$10,000 \times .05 = \$500$ Discount sent to you

$10,000 - \$500 = \$9500$ Net cost

$500 \div \$9500 = 5.3\%$ True yield on an annual basis

Also, you can take the $500, invest it somewhere else for the rest of the year, and further increase your income.

For federal income tax purposes, the $500 is considered ordinary income to be reported at the time the T-bill matures, not at the time you receive it. For example, if you bought a 1-year T-bill in July, 1994, you'd receive your full discount ($500) immediately. However, this amount would not be considered income until July 1995, when the T-bill matures. Therefore, the $500 would not have to be declared for tax purposes, nor taxes paid on it, until as late as April 1996. (Estimated tax is not considered in the example.)

What Happens at the Time of Maturity?

When it's time to redeem your T-bill, if you bought it through a bank or a broker, you'll follow the procedure arranged at the time of purchase. If you bought it directly from a Federal Reserve bank, the Treasury Department will make a direct deposit for you into your bank. This procedure smooths the way for you by having the interest payments and proceeds (when the security matures) automatically deposited into your account at any bank of your choosing.

If for any reason you have to cash in your T-bill before it matures and you bought it at a Federal Reserve bank, you must first transfer it to a bank or broker for sale on the open market. You will need to obtain a securities transfer request (STR) and submit it to the bank from which you bought the T-bill. The amount of proceeds will vary from day to day because the maturity value of the bill is affected by (1) interest rates prevailing on the sale date, (2) the number of days remaining before the T-bill matures, and (3) the bank or brokerage fee.

What Are Treasury Notes and Bonds?

Treasury notes, like T-bills, pay interest rates determined by auction. However, they are not sold at a discount. Instead, they pay interest every 6 months at a rate fixed at the time of purchase. In this respect, they resemble corporate bonds. Because you will be receiving interest every 6 months, if you should have a change of address (Form PD345) or a problem with any interest checks, contact Bureau of Public Debt, Dept. A, Washington, DC 20239-1000.

Treasury notes also have a longer life span than T-bills (up to 10 years from the date of issue). Notes that mature in 2 or 3 years are offered by the Treasury in minimum denominations of $5000, with $1000 increments thereafter (prior to April 1993, the increment was $5000). Those notes maturing in 5 or 10 years are sold in minimum denominations of $1000. Treasury note and bond auctions are usually held on the following schedule.

$5000 initially, $1,000 increments	2-yr.	Monthly; late in the month
	3-yr.	Quarterly; 15th of February, May, August, and November
$1000 initially, $1000 increments	5-yr.	Monthly; late in the month
	10-yr.	Quarterly; 15th of February, May, August, and November
	30-yr.	Semiannually; August and February

Like corporate bonds, Treasury notes can be bought and sold on the secondary market by both brokers and banks. The U.S. Treasury doesn't buy back Treasury notes: however, you can exchange notes of one denomination for those of another. The market price for a Treasury note will fluctuate, depending on changes in interest rates. You can find current prices in the financial pages of your newspaper (see Figure 19.2).

However, the actual price you'll pay a broker—or the amount you'll receive when selling your note—will differ from the price shown, because of the broker's fee and the slightly higher costs involved in buying or selling odd-lot amounts (which include purchases of less than $1 million worth of Treasury notes).

Treasury bonds are much like Treasury notes, with a few differences. They have the longest maturity periods—30 years—and are auctioned semiannually in August and February. The minimum investment is $1000. Treasury bonds tend to fluctuate in price on the secondary market more than Treasury notes, and so it is possible to lose on a Treasury obligation. Suppose that the $1000, 30-year Treasury bond you bought last year appears on your statement valued at only $970. What happened to the remaining $30? Nothing really, as you will get back your $1000 at maturity, so no risk is involved. But there is a risk on the secondary market (where Treasury obligations are traded) if you decide to sell the bond before it matures in 30 years. The proceeds from the sale are based on the market value of the bond, which depends on the direction of interest rates. When these rates rise, bond prices will tend to decrease. For example, if you bought a 30-year, 8 percent Treasury bond for $1000 today and in 3 years interest rates should rise to 9 percent, the market value of your T-bond would be less than the $1000 face value. The reason is that buyers would rather purchase a T-bond with a 9 percent return for the same $1000 than buy your 8 percent bond.

In November 1993, the U.S. Treasury made two major changes in the sale of Treasury notes and bonds: (1) It stopped issuing 7-year notes and (2) it began to sell only half as many 30-year bonds, issuing those only twice a year instead of the usual quarterly. To make up for this funding gap, the government decided to sell more short-term securities because of the low interest rates at that time. By getting rid of the 7-year note and eliminating two selling periods on the 30-year bond, by 1998 the government expects to trim the average maturity of Treasury borrowing by a full year. This move will save the government money while the economy is in a short-term low-interest period. However, if interest rates should escalate rapidly, the plan could backfire.

One last point. Bear in mind that Treasury obligations are actively traded in the secondary market, so they are relatively liquid. If you must sell a Treasury obligation before maturity, you'll earn interest on it up to the day of sale. Also, some Treasury bonds contain call provisions, allowing the government to redeem the bond any time within 5 years of the maturity date. For more information about any Treasury obligations, write to the Bureau of the Public Debt, Dept. A, Washington, DC 20239-1000 and request the "Treasury Direct Package." There is a wealth of information about these instruments. And on the topic of wealth, it is good to have money and the things that money can buy, but it is also good to check up once in awhile and make certain you haven't lost the things that money can't buy.

20

U.S. Savings Bonds— Safety First

Patriotism is not so much protecting the land of our ancestors as preserving the land for our children.

When I was in public school, World War II was under way and the sale of war bonds was very popular. Every adult bought them. Children could purchase, in small amounts, freedom stamps (10 cents or 25 cents) that were then pasted into a "victory book." When this booklet was filled ($18.75), it was turned into the bank and exchanged for a savings bond with a face value at maturity of $25. Well, things have certainly changed. Years ago savings bonds were purchased to help our country finance and win World War II, but today they're purchased for completely different reasons. There are currently two types of U.S. savings bonds available—the Series EE bond and the Series HH bond. Let me explain both types and provide some insight into their advantages and disadvantages as investment vehicles.

How Do EE Bonds Work?

The EE bond is a nonnegotiable security against the credit of the U.S. Treasury—nonnegotiable because once it is purchased it cannot be resold to anyone else but may be sold back only to the government at a fixed price. However, you are permitted to transfer the bonds to someone else by using Form PD3360 to register them in the person's name. This form is available at any Federal Reserve district bank. Bear in mind that when you transfer the savings bonds, all accrued interest becomes taxable to you. You may also have to pay a gift tax if the bonds are worth more than $10,000. If, upon the death of an owner, there is a surviving co-owner or beneficiary named on the bonds, the bonds do not form part of a decedent's estate for probate purposes. Subject to applicable estate or inheritance taxes, if any, they become the sole and absolute property of the survivor. Series EE bonds are sold at half their face value and are available in denominations of $100, $200, $500, $1000, $5000, and $10,000. Thus savings bonds are available for as little as $50, making them a practical choice for the investor with only a minimal amount of money to set aside.

The annual limit on the amount of Series EE bonds an individual may buy is $15,000 issue price ($30,000 face amount). This limit applies to the amount of bonds that may be purchased in the name of any one person in any one calendar year; it has no effect on cumulative holdings. Purchasing bonds in co-ownership form effectively doubles the limit, if neither co-owner has purchased other bonds.

U.S. savings bonds are easy to buy. In 1992 a new method for issuing savings bonds purchased over the counter was implemented by the Treasury. Referred to as the *regional delivery system* (RDS), it consolidates responsibility for the inscription and issuance of savings bonds with the Federal Reserve banks. Banks, savings and loans, and other financial institutions continue to receive bond purchase applications and payments from their customers. However, instead of each financial institution issuing bonds directly, with RDS the purchase information is forwarded to a Federal Reserve bank, which issues and mails the bonds to customers, usually within 2 or 3 weeks. If you like buying savings bonds as last-minute gifts, the bank will give you a gift certificate.

You can also buy savings bonds on a regular basis through your employer's payroll-deduction plan. This is a very valuable service for those who find it hard to save unless forced to do so. With payroll deduction, the money to buy your bonds is taken out of your salary check before you get it, thus reducing the pain involved in saving and eliminating the temptation to spend the money rather than put it aside.

Years ago, U.S. savings bonds paid a notoriously low rate of interest. This now has changed. In 1982, the federal government realized that it was necessary to make savings bonds more competitive with higher-yielding investments such as money market funds. Therefore, the fixed-interest schedule formerly used for savings bonds was changed to a variable rate. Each May 1 and November 1, the Treasury computes the average daily market yield on 5-year Treasury marketable securities during the preceding 6 months. The savings bond rate is set at 85 percent of the market average. At the end of 5 years, the average of the 10 semiannual rates, compounded semiannually, determines a bond's 5-year yield. If a bond is held for 6 years, 12 semiannual rates are averaged, and so on. The minimum rate, effective March 1, 1993, is 4 percent. Bonds bought after this date and held for less than 5 years will also earn interest at this rate. Before March 1993, bonds earned a graduated minimum rate (4.16 percent for 6 months and progressively more until 6 percent was reached after 5 years).

Another factor to consider is the method of calculation of older bonds. These bonds, issued prior to November 1986, earn a guaranteed minimum of 7.5 percent. Although they pay interest for 30 years, the guaranteed minimum is good only for the original maturity period—in this case, approximately 10 years. After that time period, the original minimum expires and the new 4 percent minimum takes effect. For example, if a bond was bought in 1983, the new calculation for 1994 would be 10 years at 7.5 percent minimum and 1 year at 4 percent; for 1995, 7.5 percent minimum for 10 years and 4 percent for 2 years; and so forth.

The new variable interest rate is a boon to investors

because when market interest rates rise, the owner of U.S. savings bonds will now benefit from the higher yields rather than being locked into a low fixed rate as before. The 4 percent minimum rate will protect the investor in case interest rates take a dramatic plunge. For example, if the 5-year Treasury average is 7 percent, your EE bonds will pay 5.95 percent (85 percent of 7 percent). However, if the Treasury rate falls to 3.5 percent, you'll still receive the minimum 4 percent on your EE bonds. To find out the latest interest rates on these bonds, call 1-800-US BONDS.

Thus, U.S. savings bonds, while still not the highest-paying investment around, do offer a respectable yield along with their unmatched safety—safety not only for their guarantee of principal and interest, but also for their repayment should they be stolen, lost, or destroyed. If any of these situations occurs, bonds can be replaced by notifying the Bureau of Public Debt, 200 Third Street, Parkersburg, WV 26101-1328.

How Do You Redeem Savings Bonds?

No matter on what day of the month you buy your EE bonds, you will be credited with interest for the full month. This means that even if you buy the bonds on the last day of the month, you will get credit for interest beginning on the first day of the month. That rule of buying applies no matter when you purchase the bonds. However, when it comes to redeeming, different rules apply depending on the purchase date. Bonds bought before March 1993 and held for less than 30 months will have their interest credited on the first day of each month for the previous month. For example, if you cashed in your bonds on August 31, you would receive interest through July 31 only. But if you could wait just one more day and cash the bonds in on September 1, you would be credited with interest for the month of August also. If you held the bonds for more than 30 months, interest would be credited every 6 months, starting from the month of purchase. For example, if you bought bonds 10 years ago dur-

Table 20.1. SAVINGS BOND EXTENSION TABLE		
Series	Dates of issue	Interest-bearing life
E*	May 1941– November 1965	40 years
	December 1965– June 1980	30 years
EE	All issues	30 years
Notes	All issues	30 years
H*	All issues	30 years
HH	All issues	20 years

*Some issues have already reached final maturity and have ceased earning interest.

ing the month of January, you would have to wait until July 1 to be certain of receiving interest for the full 6-month period (January to July). If you redeemed the bonds even a day too soon, you would lose 6 months of interest. The following rule should be easy to understand: "In whatever month you purchase a savings bond (the month is stamped on the bond), consider that month as the first month of a 6-month cycle and sell the bond in the seventh month."

New rules apply on bonds bought after March 1, 1993, since the interest will be credited on the first of each month no matter how long you hold the bonds. Therefore, timing becomes less important. Also, the Treasury Department has made an extension schedule for savings bonds showing the interest-bearing lives of all outstanding issues. (See Table 20.1.)

How Do Taxes Affect Savings Bonds?

The interest payout on U.S. savings bonds is tax-exempt at the state and local level but is subject to inheritance and estate taxes levied by states and localities. It is tax-deferred at the federal level. That is, the interest you receive is paid in one lump sum at the time of redemption and is fully taxable in that year. You can avoid a heavy tax liability by buying savings bonds in your child's name and treating each year's interest income as reportable as earned. Here's how it works. File a tax return for your youngster in the year you buy the bond. This shows the IRS that you intend to report the interest income from the bond annually rather than in total upon redemption. You can get yearly interest rates from tables published by the Treasury. As long as the income generated from the bond is under $1200 (assuming no income from other sources), it will be taxed at the child's lower tax rate if he or she is under age 14. After age 14, all income, regardless of amount, is taxable at the child's rate. But note that once the child elects to declare the EE income annually, he or she must do so with all future bonds purchased for 5 years. And bear in mind that the youngster is entitled to the standard deduction because a separate tax return (Form 1040) has been filed in his or her name. If the bond interest is the major source of income, he or she will pay little or no tax on this income. Also, the parents will not lose their child's personal exemption, as they are still permitted to take the child as a deduction on their own return.

If you intend to use this method to save on taxes, be sure to take two precautions: First, save copies of your child's income tax forms until you've redeemed the bonds. Second, don't put your name or anyone else's on the bond as co-owner. The instrument must be in the child's name only, so that the child is presumed to be the owner no matter who paid for the bond. This tax-saving technique is most appropriate for use with bonds that are intended for savings to benefit the child—a college tuition fund, for example.

What Role Do Bonds Play in Plans for College?

On January 1, 1990, a new education savings bond program began. Known as the Technical and Miscellaneous Revenue

Act of 1988 (TAMRA '88), it permitted qualified taxpayers
to exclude from their gross income all or a part of the interest earned on savings bonds bought after that date. This tax-
free income (federal, state, and local) is permitted if the proceeds of the bonds are used only for the child's college fees,
which do not include room, board, or books.

It sounds great, but is it really? The conditions that must
be met are quite numerous and will in essence disallow this
tax loophole for most people. In order to get this tax-free
income, the following conditions must prevail:

1. The child cannot own the bond. The bond must be
   owned by the parents, who must be over 24 years of age.

2. If your "modified" adjusted gross income is more than
   $60,000, or $40,000 if you are an individual filer (this
   income level is considered at the time of redemption and
   not at the purchase date), the bonds will begin to lose
   their tax-free nature. A portion of the interest can be still
   considered tax-exempt over these levels, but couples
   whose income exceeds $90,000 or individual filers whose
   income exceeds $55,000 will not be able to get the tax-free
   advantage. These income limits will rise each year with
   the inflation rate, but you will not know what they will be
   until you finally redeem the bonds. The problem is obvious. You could invest money in these savings bonds for
   years and then find out when your child enters college
   that you fail to qualify because your income has outpaced
   inflation. In other words, if you finally "make it financially," you will be penalized. To add insult to injury, you
   must be married when you redeem the bonds, since only
   couples who file a joint return will get the exemption. If
   you are divorced, you will have to pay taxes unless your
   income is under the individual-filer limit.

3. Your yearly expenses for college tuition must be more
   than what you receive in the same year from the bonds
   you redeem. For example, if you receive $8000 for the
   bonds, $4000 of which is interest, and you spend $6000
   in college costs, you will be allowed only $3000 as an

exemption (75 percent of the $4000 interest). The 75 percent figure derives from the fact that only $6000 of the $8000 (that is, three-fourths, or 75 percent) has been used for acceptable college expenses. Therefore, it is important that you attempt to balance what you receive in bonds each year with your annual tuition costs.

4. You do not have to declare how you intend to use the money from the savings bonds when you purchase them, but you must be ready to show evidence that the money was used for educational purposes when you cash in the bonds.

5. The standard limitation of $30,000 face value or $15,000 purchase price (or $60,000 and $30,000 for husband and wife holding bonds as co-owners) in bonds per year applies to the education bond program as well as to all EE issues. However, there is no limit to the amount of bonds that can be accumulated for educational expenses over time.

For more information about savings bonds for college education write to the Office of Public Affairs, U.S. Savings Bond Division, Department CT, Washington, DC 20226.

How Do HH Bonds Work?

Up to this point, we've been discussing EE bonds only. The HH bonds are different in several ways. Unlike EE bonds, HH bonds pay interest on a semiannual basis. Therefore, the interest income is taxable as it is earned throughout the life of the bond. HH bonds mature in 20 years, pay 6 percent (if bought before March 1, 1993; 4% after that date), and are available in denominations of $500, $1000, $5000, and $10,000.

You can't buy HH bonds for cash. They can be acquired only in exchange for (1) EE bonds, or (2) the older E bonds. You have 1 year from the final maturity date of your Series E bonds to transfer them to Series HH. By making this transfer, you can continue to defer taxes. Therefore, if your income is likely to drop over the next 20 years (the life of HH bonds), you will benefit from this deferral. These exchanges can be made by any of the 12 Federal Reserve banks and their 24 branches, or by using Form PD3253, which can be secured at any bank.

Any month after June is a good time to make the switch. For example, looking toward the future, if you swap EE bonds for HH bonds during July 1995, the first payment of HH interest to you won't be made until January 1996. This means that you will not have to declare the income until 1997 when you file your 1996 return.

Why would anyone turn in their EE bonds to get HH bonds? It's a way of stretching out and so limiting the income tax liability that goes along with the lump-sum interest payout characteristic of EE bonds. The interest payable on your mature EE bonds isn't taxable at the time you exchange them for HH bonds. Instead, the amount of interest accumulated on the EE bonds is stamped on the face of the HH bonds. That amount is not taxable as current income until you cash in your HH bonds, which may not happen for quite a while—not until after retirement, for example, at which time your income and tax bracket could be lower. If you're planning on retiring fairly soon, it's a good idea to exchange your EE bonds for HH bonds rather than simply cashing them in. And on the topic of retirement, remember it is always better to retire too soon than too late.

21

Zero Investment

Dig a well before you are thirsty.

The zero coupon bond is a unique financial tool which has become, over the years, an increasingly popular instrument for long-term investment. As you will see in the following pages, zero coupon bonds have some definite advantages over other types of long-term investments. They have become an excellent choice for individual retirement accounts (IRAs), 401(k) plans, Keogh and other pension funds, and most certainly for a child's college savings. They are therefore an ideal investment for those of you who are more concerned about "outcome" than about "income."

How Does the Zero Coupon Bond Work?

Bonds are debt obligations issued by a corporation or by a federal, state, or local government agency. When you buy a bond (usually at face value), you are buying a promise from the issuing institution to pay the amount of the face of the bond at maturity. However, unlike the traditional bonds mentioned in earlier chapters, "zeros" are sold at a price well below the face value. Thus, these bonds are appealing to the small investor because they can be bought far cheaper than ordinary debt obligations. The discount is usually from 50 to 75 percent. For example, a zero with a face value of

$1000 (at 8 percent) may sell for just $456. You pay $456 today; at the time of maturity—10 years—you can redeem the bond for its full $1000 face value. The extra $544 paid on redemption is the accumulated 10 years' worth of interest on your $456 investment.

During the life of the zero, you clip no coupons and receive no interest payments (hence the name "zero coupon bonds"). The entire interest payout comes at once—upon redemption.

Table 21.1 shows the price for a $1000 zero coupon bond under various interest rates and maturity dates. Naturally, the longer the term of the bond and the higher the interest rate, the greater the discount at which the bond is sold. Note that the amounts are rounded to the nearest dollar.

If you're still in your twenties or thirties, you may purchase a big chunk of retirement money very cheaply by buying a long-term zero right now. For example, at an 8 percent interest rate, you may buy a zero redeemable at $1000 in 30 years for under $100. It's hard to imagine a better buy than that.

Table 21.1. THE COST OF A $1000 ZERO COUPON BOND

Interest rate	Maturity date and cost*					
	5 years	10 years	15 years	20 years	25 years	30 years
6%	$744	$544	$412	$307	$228	$170
7	709	502	356	255	179	127
8	676	456	308	208	141	95
9	644	415	267	172	111	71
10	614	377	231	142	87	54

*Actual price can vary because of availability, fees, and other factors affecting bond prices.

What Advantages Do Zeros Offer as an Investment?

Zero coupon bonds offer several distinct advantages. Zeros have *call protection,* meaning that it is unlikely that they will be called in for early redemption by the issuing company if interest rates should fall. (There'd be no advantage to the corporation in prepaying the interest on zeros unless there were special call provisions in the agreement.) As you are aware, we are presently experiencing major calls in bonds. Thus be certain to find out whether the bond you wish to purchase is callable and if so, ask about its "yield to call." Yield to call means that you will be guaranteed a set return if the bond is called in early. Also, if interest rates in the market should fall, with a conventional bond the interest payments you receive would have to be reinvested at the lower existing rate. You avoid this when you purchase zero coupon bonds because the interest is reinvested at the fixed rate (which was higher than the prevailing rate) at which you purchased them.

Zeros also offer liquidity. If, for some reason you need to sell your bond before maturity, you can sell it on the so-called secondary market at the current rate. This may produce a gain or loss depending upon interest rates at the time of the sale. For example, if interest rates are higher at the time you dispose of the bonds, you will take a loss. However, a lower interest rate will yield you a profit. And speaking about interest rates, another advantage of zeros is that you avoid the roller coaster ups and downs of interest rates if a bond is kept to maturity. As stated above, the value of a bond will rise if interest rates fall and will drop in value if interest rates rise. With zero bonds, no matter how much their value may fluctuate and fall, at maturity the bond will be redeemed at its face value. This gives you the assurance of knowing exactly what you will receive at a certain time in the future.

Most important, zeros adapt themselves very well to a variety of personal financial plans. Because you know exactly how much money you'll be receiving for your investment and exactly when the payout will occur, you can make long-range plans on the basis of your investment in zeros. Thus, they make an excellent choice for your individual retirement account (IRA) or Keogh plan investment, allowing you to accumulate tax-deferred interest at a fixed rate until retirement. This is because the annual earnings of the IRA or Keogh (known as "imputed interest") are not subject to annual tax until they are withdrawn.

Are Zero Coupon Bonds a Good Investment Vehicle for Education?

Zero coupon bonds are also an excellent way of saving for your child's college tuition. That just-born baby is certainly a joy today but financially a major cost problem years from now. Someone has described a baby as making your days shorter, nights longer, bankrolls smaller, the past forgotten, and the future worth living for. However, it has been estimated that the average cost of 4 years of college could be as high as $200,000 at an Ivy League school by the time that newborn reaches 18 years of age.

You can invest in zeros which will mature at the time your child is ready for school and, at the same time, greatly reduce the tax bite on the interest if the transaction is done properly. Remember, under the Tax Reform Act only the first $1200 of your child's unearned income will be taxed at his or her low rate, with the first $600 being exempt (because of the standard deduction). This means that by reporting the interest each year on the child's return, you will get that exemption 18 times (assuming an 18-year bond), for a total of $10,800. However, if the interest were to be reported in one lump sum only (as with some instruments), you would be able to use the $600 exemption only once. Also, by declaring the tax each year, you do not have to concern yourself about having a taxable lump-sum amount come due just when you are about to pay for your child's college tuition.

One more point on this topic. Make absolutely certain that the zeros mature when the child is past the age of 14, since all income will be subject to the child's lower rate. Before age 14, all income (subject to the $1200 limitation) is taxable at the parent's rate. To avoid any tax to the child, consider the zero coupon municipal bond after annual earnings of $1200 of annual interest income has been reached.

What Are the Disadvantages of the Zero Coupon Bond?

Zero coupon bonds do have some disadvantages. The degree of risk is one. If the company issuing the bonds is no longer solvent at the time of maturity, you may lose your entire investment. The possibility of default is a serious consideration with bonds of every kind, but the problem is especially significant with zeros. This is because you receive all interest payments at one time, upon maturity, whereas with other types of bonds you receive interest on a regular basis throughout the life of the bond.

A second disadvantage involves the markup that brokers add to the wholesale price of the bonds. The cost to purchase a zero is much higher (in percentage terms) than that of ordinary bonds because of the broker's markup, which is based on face value rather than cost. For example, a $30 commission on an ordinary $1000 (face value) bond is only 3 percent but on the much smaller price of a zero the same $30 commission would be quite high (on a $300 zero it would be 10 percent). It is very difficult for an investor to determine what the markup is on zero coupon bonds because the bonds are sold "net." Brokerage houses buy them at wholesale and resell them to the general public at retail prices. The markup, which is used instead of a sales commission, will increase the price of buying the zero and will reduce the price you get when you sell.

The only way to know whether your broker is charging you a fair price is to shop around. Call other brokerage houses to see what the competition has to offer. Remember that the larger the broker's markup, the more the bond will cost, leaving you with a smaller "yield." Also, prices of zeros change everyday, so if you are seeking the best rate, do all your shopping on the *same* day in order to compare fairly.

When comparing brokers, ask each of them the following questions:

1. How much will I have to invest in order to get the bond (zero) that I want?

2. How much will that investment be worth at maturity?

3. What is the effective yield to maturity?

The broker who can give you the lowest figure for question (1) and the highest figures for (2) and (3) will be getting you your money's worth. As a humorous sidelight, those investors who were hurt in the market crash of 1987 and 1989 felt that people selling stocks are called brokers because after you take their advice you are.

A third disadvantage involves taxes. Although you receive no cash payments during the life of the zero coupon bond, you are taxed as if you do, because interest on a zero coupon bond must be reported to the IRS each year. After 18 years, a zero bought for $200 might grow to $1000 at maturity. To report the $800 interest, you do not take $\frac{1}{18}$ of it ($44 each year), but report the interest as it actually accrues. During the first year, a $200 investment earning 8 percent would produce approximately $16. In the second year, your investment would not be $200 but $216 ($200 + $16), and $17.28 would be the interest that year. You do not have to personally compute this every year; you will receive a notice from the issuer or your broker informing you of the amount of interest to report to the IRS. The tax on this "invisible interest," also known as "phantom income," can be considered a major drawback of zero coupon bonds, because you are forced to pay tax on income you haven't received and will not receive for many years. To avoid this problem, look into the *zero coupon municipal bond.*

What Is a Zero Coupon Municipal Bond?

The zero coupon municipal bond performs the same as a corporate zero coupon bond except that it is issued by a state or local government agency. Maturities range from 7 to 30 years. Because it is a municipal bond, the interest you earn is exempt from all federal taxes and, in many cases, if the bond is issued within your state, from state and local taxes as well. The amount you receive at maturity is considered tax-free income which has accrued annually from the time of the issuance of the bonds.

Those attracted to zero coupon bonds should also consider one more alternative: zeros issued by the U.S. Treasury, the safest of the three types. These are sometimes called by other names, such as *stripped Treasuries,* a name given by brokerage houses which "strip" smaller investment units from large Treasury bonds for sale to investors.

The most valuable feature of the zero coupon bond is that it lets you know exactly how much money you'll have at a particular future date. This facilitates financial planning for the years to come. Tell your broker when you'd like your bonds to mature, and he or she can let you know when zeros that meet your future needs are available. And on the topic of the future, the future is that time when you wish you'd done what you aren't doing now.

PART 2

Financial Planning for the Future

22

Planning Your Retirement— An Overview

Retirement takes all the fun out of Saturdays.

In the following chapters, various retirement plans are discussed. Whether you are employed by a corporation or a government agency, are self-employed, or are working part time, some of the options explained in the following pages will affect your future financial plans.

How Do Lump-Sum Distributions Work?

Every day, for various reasons, people receive large lump-sum distributions representing the accumulated value of their pension plans. This may occur when you retire, or it may occur sooner if you become disabled, if you leave your present employer, or if the company decides to terminate your pension plan. In any case, when you receive such a lump-sum distribution, you face a problem: How do you minimize the taxes on this often sizable payment?

There are basically two solutions: (1) 5-year forward averaging for tax purposes and (2) an individual retirement account (IRA) rollover. Let's consider both of these techniques.

What Is the 5-Year Forward-Averaging Plan?

You may be acquainted with ordinary income averaging, which is a way of reducing your income taxes for a year in which your income is markedly higher than in previous years. Five-year forward averaging is slightly different in that it allows your lump-sum distribution to be taxed at a different, lower rate than your other income. Here's how it works.

When you use 5-year forward averaging, your lump-sum distribution is taxed as if you were receiving it in five equal annual payments. For each of the 5 years, you pay taxes on just one-fifth of the total distribution. Furthermore, the tax on each installment is computed as though the lump-sum distribution were your only source of income for the year, which is then added to your other income tax payments for the year. The tax is likely to be far less than it would be if it were computed as part of your entire year's income. Under the Tax Reform Act (TRA), if you were age 50 by January 1986, you can use 10 years instead of 5 years in computing forward averaging, if you use specific tax rate tables.

In order for you to use either method, your distribution must come from a qualified plan in which you have been enrolled for at least 5 years, the sum must represent your entire interest in the plan, and you must be at least age $59\frac{1}{2}$.

If you decide to forward-average (under either a 5- or 10-year plan), the tax law requires you to use the method on all other lump sums you receive in the same year from any other tax-deferred plan. In other words, you cannot forward-average one lump sum and roll over others into an IRA.

What Is an IRA Rollover?

Another way to reduce the taxes on your lump-sum distribution is to roll it over—that is, reinvest it—in an IRA. This must be done within 60 days of receiving the distribution or you will lose the tax-shelter status otherwise conferred by the IRA. You don't have to pay any current income taxes on the distribution amount if you deposit it in an IRA, nor will you owe taxes on the income which accumulates in the account. The IRA funds become taxable only upon withdrawal, which may begin after you reach age $59\frac{1}{2}$ and must begin by age $70\frac{1}{2}$. See Chapter 23 for specific rulings on IRA rollovers.

Which Method—5-Year Averaging or IRA Rollover—Is Better?

The answer to this question depends on your personal financial situation. If you plan to retire and liquidate your IRA in a short time—say, 4 years or less—then the 5-year forward-averaging method is likely to save you more money. This is because, once you begin withdrawing your IRA funds, the money is usually taxed at a higher rate than that called for under 5-year averaging.

Another consideration is the level of income you expect to enjoy after retirement. If you expect your income to decline sharply upon retirement, then an IRA rollover plan is probably your best choice. Chances are that, under those circumstances, the taxes you'll pay when withdrawing your IRA funds will be relatively low. On the other hand, if income from other sources will keep you in a fairly high tax bracket when you retire, then the 5-year forward averaging plan is best. Pay the low 5-year averaging rate and invest the distribution amount in an appropriate tax-saving instrument such as municipal bonds. As with most financial decisions, several factors must be taken into account, and only you can decide which is most important to you.

How Does Early Retirement Play a Role in the Various Plans?

There is a story of a beautiful bird who was powerful and free. It had magnificent, colorful plumage, of which it was very proud. One day the bird decided to pluck its feathers, one by one, in order to make a nest in which it could rest in comfort and security. Now it cannot fly.

Don't consider retiring until you are both financially and emotionally ready. Why? Because people have not been properly prepared for retirement in America. We spend a third of our lifetime preparing for a career,but almost no time in preparing for the period afterward. There are thousands of books and pamphlets on retirement, but most do not cover the most important consideration: the feeling of being retired. Today's unanswered question seems to be not so much what happens physically to people when they retire as what happens to them emotionally. The American public, the government, and the medical profession put more effort into helping folks reach old age than in helping them enjoy it. Can you imagine filling 10 hours a day (3650 hours a year) in leisure? That huge amount of time hangs over every retired person like unspent capital.

So be very careful when you decide at what age you will leave the work force. The decision to retire will be based on your financial status, and careful planning is mandatory. For example, people who are nearing retirement or have begun retirement with a fixed asset base may be concerned whether their money will last as long as it will be needed. If you are forced to dip into your principal in order to make ends meet, Table 22.1 may be of great help to you. It shows how long your money will last if you must draw from it at a rate faster than it is growing. As an illustration, suppose your assets are earning an 8 percent annual return and you must withdraw 15 percent of your principal each year in order to live comfortably in retirement. As shown in the table, your money should last approximately 10 years.

What Are the Implications of the 1994 Tax Rules?

The year 1994 changed a great deal of tax planning. It is impossible to attempt to write here about the complicated and voluminous amount of legislation that was passed. A few highlights that can affect most Americans follow.

Table 22.1. EARNINGS AND WITHDRAWALS										
If principal is earning at this rate	And you are withdrawing at this rate									
	16%	15%	14%	13%	12%	11%	10%	9%	8%	7%	6%
12%	12	14	17	23	Here's how many years your
11	11	13	15	18	24		principal will last
10	10	12	13	15	19	25				
9	10	11	12	14	16	20	27			
8	9	10	11	12	14	17	21	28		
7	9	9	10	11	13	15	18	22	31	
6	8	9	10	11	12	13	16	19	24	33
5	8	8	9	10	11	12	14	17	20	26	37

1. Once the level of $44,000 (joint) or $33,000 (individual) of provisional income (taxable income plus tax-exempt interest income and 50 percent of social security benefits) is reached, the excess income will be subject to a rate of 85 percent of social security benefits instead of the 50 percent—$32,000 (joint) and $25,000 (individual)—this past year. In other words, a second tier of taxation is created once last year's limits have been reached. (See Chapter 25.)

2. If you earn over $162,700 (joint) or ($108,450 (individual) of adjusted gross income (AGI), your total itemized deductions are reduced by 3 percent of the excess, with exceptions for medical, casualty, and theft. Personal exemptions are phased out at a rate of 2 percent for every $2500 by which your AGI exceeds $162,700 (joint) or $108,450 (individual). This rule is now permanent.

3. If you earn over $135,000, you will be charged with the 1.45 percent Medicare tax (self-employed is 2.9 percent). In 1993, there was no tax above the $135,000 figure.

4. For income earned in 1994 and after, a new top income tax rate of 36 percent has been established for incomes of $140,000 (joint) or $115,000 (individual). In addition, a surtax of 10 percent is placed on any taxable income of more than $250,000. In effect, this 10 percent surtax creates a new tax bracket of 39.6 percent; and if you consider some of the other changes mentioned above, your true effective tax rate could exceed 45 percent. Adding state and local taxes to this rate, 50 percent is no longer an impossible tax-bracket figure.

5. For those who pay estimated income tax, the rule now adds the stipulation that taxpayers with AGI over $150,000 must assume that their income will rise 10 percent. This means that you must prepay either 90 percent of your current tax or 110 percent of the previous year's tax.

The following chapters should be of value to you in determining the various option plans for your retirement. And on the topic of retirement, before you decide to retire, take a week off and watch daytime TV.

23
The IRA

*You can plan for tomorrow today but you
can't plan for today tomorrow.*

The *individual retirement account* (*IRA*) is a method of investing originally designed to help individuals not covered by
company pension plans save for their retirement. On
January 1, 1982, the law governing IRAs was changed to
make them available to anyone with earned income (wages,
fees) whether or not the individual was covered by a company pension plan. The law was changed again in January
1987, and still again in 1993, to limit the amount deductible
from your income tax.

How Does the IRA Work?

First, some basic ground rules. Your IRA is a savings account
containing funds that can be invested in any of a number of
different financial instruments. (I'll offer some guidelines on
your options in a moment.) By law, you may contribute to
your IRA up to 100 percent of the first $2000 that you earn
each year. If a husband and wife are both working, they can
establish an IRA and contribute up to $2000 per year to each
account, for a family total of $4000. If one spouse does not
work, up to $2250 may be contributed, with a maximum of
$2000 in one account. Many advertisers are touting the fact
that a $2000 annual deposit into an IRA (at 10 percent) by a
25-year-old would be worth nearly $1 million ($973,704)

Year	Interest rate			
	6%	8%	10%	12%
1	$2,120	$2,160	$2,200	$2,240
5	11,951	12,672	13,431	14,230
10	27,943	31,291	35,062	39,309
15	49,345	58,649	69,900	83,507
20	77,985	98,846	126,005	161,397
25	116,313	157,909	216,364	298,668
30	167,603	244,692	361,887	540,585
35	236,242	372,204	596,254	966,927
40	328,095	599,562	973,704	1,718,285

Table 23.1. VALUE OF PRINCIPAL FOR $2000 YEARLY IRA CONTRIBUTION

when the person reached age 65. Table 23.1 shows the value for different years and rate yields for a constant $2000 annual contribution. The figures are impressive.

But here is where the rules changed under the Tax Reform Act (TRA). If you or your spouse is considered an active participant in a qualified pension plan (even if you do not as yet have vested rights), you will have limits imposed on your IRA contribution. You can still contribute up to $2000 as long as your adjusted gross income (AGI) is not more than $25,000 (individual) or $40,000 (joint). If you are an individual filer earning between $25,000 and $35,000 or a joint filer earning between $40,000 and $50,000, your deductible amount of $2000 will be reduced by 20 percent of your income over $25,000 (individual) and $40,000 (joint). For example, a taxpayer (individual) earning $28,000 may deduct, for tax purposes, only $1400 of the $2000 contribution—that is, $2000 less $600 (20% × $3000, the excess over $25,000). Table 23.2 shows the maximum deduction you may take if your income falls within the mid-range.

Table 23.2. MAXIMUM IRA DEDUCTIONS FOR MID-RANGE INCOMES

Individual	Joint	Maximum IRA deduction
$25,000	$40,000	$2000
26,000	41,000	1800
27,000	42,000	1600
28,000	43,000	1400
29,000	44,000	1200
30,000	45,000	1000
31,000	46,000	800
32,000	47,000	600
33,000	48,000	400
34,000	49,000	200
35,000	50,000	0

One more point. It is very important that you make your IRA contribution in the beginning of the year. Over the long run, the tax deferral you get from the compounding of your earnings on that money can actually be more valuable than your IRA contribution. If you earn 6 percent on your $2000 annual contribution, the $120 interest on the money you earn each year is compounded from the beginning of the year. If you wait until the end of the year, you will lose a whole year's compounded interest.

What Are the Tax Consequences of the IRA?

The money you contribute to your IRA is deducted from your income for tax purposes, providing immediate tax benefits, and is called a *deductible contribution*. Although individual filers in a pension plan with incomes over $35,000 and joint filers in a pension plan with incomes over $50,000 cannot make deductible contributions, they still can make nondeductible contributions up to $2000, with the earnings from that amount accumulating tax-free. These nondeductible contributions can be withdrawn without penalty, but the interest earned on them, if withdrawn, is subject to tax and a possible early withdrawal penalty if the taxpayer has not yet reached age 59½. Under the TRA there is a special treatment for deductible and nondeductible withdrawals. The TRA requires that you combine all IRA monies (both deductible and nondeductible) and pay tax on a prorated portion withdrawn. For example, a taxpayer who has $10,000 in IRAs ($8000 in a deductible account and $2000 in a new, nondeductible one) must lump them together for computation of withdrawal. If the taxpayer takes out $2000, only 20 percent, or $400, would be considered to come originally from the nondeductible IRA contribution. The balance of $1600 would be considered to be from the deductible IRA and would be subject to tax.

What Are the Rules for IRA Distributions?

Since the IRA was created specifically to make it easier for working people to save for their retirement, there are built-in restrictions on your access to IRA funds. You can begin withdrawing your IRA money without penalty after reaching age 59½. If you must withdraw the money before that time, you will have to pay an extra 10 percent tax on the amount you withdraw as a penalty, unless you're disabled.

One important point must be noted at this time. An individual may withdraw funds from an IRA without penalty (before age 59½) as long as the individual makes equal withdrawals each year in predetermined amounts. This method of withdrawal (called *annuitizing*) is designed to deplete the amount of money in the IRA over the life expectancy of the person. To those individuals who wish to retire in their fifties, this withdrawal option is of great benefit because it allows them to supplement their income until their social security benefits begin at age 62. Also, parents can now tap their IRAs before age $59\frac{1}{2}$ to help pay the high costs of education for their children.

What is important is that the IRA funds are able to be withdrawn under the annuity plan for any purpose without any justification needed. Even if the person was not able or eligible for the $2000 contribution, proceeds from pension plans, for example, can be rolled over into the IRA and the withdrawal plan option can be utilized for these funds. Also, and most important, once the yearly withdrawals begin, they must continue at the same rate for at least 5 years. A change after that period of time is permitted as long as the person is over $59\frac{1}{2}$. Therefore, a 55-year-old would be able to (1) stop making annual withdrawals, (2) change the amount of withdrawal, or (3) withdraw the entire balance at age 60. Just remember that by tapping the IRA funds, you are reducing the basic financial structure for your retirement years and also your ability to have your money grow through tax-deferred savings.

The penalty for early withdrawal deters many young people from opening IRAs. When you're 25 years old, $59\frac{1}{2}$ may seem an eternity away, and more than 30 years may seem like an impossibly long time to tie up your money. However, the effects of the penalty aren't nearly as severe as you might think. Because of the tax benefits derived both at the time of the contribution and during the accumulation of tax-free interest, IRA accounts become profitable fairly quickly even when the penalty for early withdrawal is taken into account. With 5 or 6 years of compounding, your income will compensate for the withdrawal penalty. After that time, even if you incur the 10 percent penalty, you will have increased your money faster than otherwise possible because of the tax benefits. Therefore, don't let the early withdrawal penalty discourage you unduly. An IRA is still a highly beneficial investment to have.

When you reach age $70\frac{1}{2}$, you must begin to take money out of your IRA. The first year, however, the government gives you a grace period until April 1 of the following year. After that first year, your withdrawal must be made by December 31. Remember, that if you take advantage of the delay in the first year, you will have to take 2 years' worth of withdrawals, which could push you into a higher tax bracket and make your social security benefits more exposed to tax. The minimum amount of withdrawal each year is based on your life expectancy or, if a beneficiary is named, on the joint life expectancy of both. To compute the withdrawal, you divide the amount in the IRA by the appropriate life expectancy figure. At age 70, a life expectancy of 15 years would mean $\frac{1}{15}$ of your total IRA balance. In years to follow, you can reduce the original expectancy by 1 year ($\frac{1}{14}$, $\frac{1}{13}$, $\frac{1}{12}$, etc.). This is known as "term certain." Another method available is to recalculate ("annual recalculation" method) the number of years of life expectancy each year. Remember, though, that once you choose a method, you must stay with it.

However, if one spouse dies, only the survivor's life expectancy can be used. When both parties die, the entire balance of the IRA must be paid out within a year to whoever is designated. That lump sum could produce a major tax bill for your beneficiary. By using the "term-certain" method, the beneficiary gets the money in small amounts annually, just as the maker of the IRA would have received.

No matter which method is chosen, you must make a definite decision. If you do not, for example, let the government know whether you wish your IRA money paid out over individual or joint life expectancies by the year you reach age $70\frac{1}{2}$, IRS will make that choice for you through the individual life expectancy method. Also, you will lose your choice again if your IRA does not specify "term-certain." IRS will make the distribution using the "annual recalculation" method.

A change in the law allows you to extend your IRA withdrawal period to cover the combined life expectancy of you and your spouse. This figure will usually be higher than the life expectancy of either husband or wife. For example, as an assumption, a 70-year-old man is expected to live 12 years, a 70-year-old woman, 15 years. However, one or the other might be expected to survive for 18 years. Therefore, the 70-year-old couple can use the 18-year life expectancy figure as the basis of their withdrawals if they wish—and they can recalculate their combined life expectancy each year as well.

What Happens If You Die before You Become Eligible to Use Your IRA Funds?

There are several possibilities. When you start an IRA, you designate a beneficiary. When you die, your beneficiary, if it is a spouse, may choose any of the following options:

1. The spouse can withdraw IRA funds as a lump sum which would be taxable during that year.
2. The spouse can take yearly distributions based on his or her life expectancy.
3. The spouse can use a portion of the money for current needs and roll over the balance.
4. The spouse can convert the IRA into his or her own account. The new owner will have all the rights and obligations of the former owner.

Most spouses choose to roll over the money left to them into their own IRA. However, if the beneficiary is not a spouse, he or she has only 5 years to take all the money out of the account and cannot roll the funds into an IRA.

What Investment Options Are Available for an IRA?

When you invest in an IRA, the law requires that a trustee be named to administer the account. The trustee must file reports with you and with the federal government. Typical

IRA trustees include commercial and savings banks, savings and loan institutions, brokerage houses, insurance companies, and other types of investment firms.

As for the type of investment, any of a wide range of choices may be suitable for your IRA, depending on your age and financial status and the degree of risk you wish to take. The only restrictions on IRA investments are these: You may not invest your IRA funds in collectibles, such as postage stamps, coins (except certain U.S. gold and silver coins), antiques, or art; you may not invest your IRA funds in life insurance contracts; and you may not make an investment in which you have a direct interest, as, for example, if you were to buy a home with IRA funds and then rent it from the IRA account.

Here are some of the most popular investment choices for IRA accounts:

Certificates of deposit: An IRA bank account usually takes the form of a certificate of deposit with a minimum term of 18 months. Rates may be fixed in advance or variable. If the rate is variable, find out just how it is set and how often it is adjusted—weekly, monthly, or whatever. In general, the most conservative investment strategy is to invest for the shortest available term.

Stocks and bonds: If you wish, you can deposit your IRA money with a stockbroker, who will act as your trustee. However, you direct the account yourself: You make your own investment decisions and you can buy and sell stocks and bonds, moving your funds from one investment to another, without incurring any taxes on the money.

Mutual funds: You can deposit your IRA money in a mutual fund, and so invest not in a few self-selected stocks but in a managed portfolio of many issues put together by a brokerage firm. You may wish to choose a broker who offers a "family of funds" of different types among which you are free to switch your investment from time to time without charge or penalty. Also, remember that there's no need to invest in any of the special tax-exempt mutual funds; your IRA investment is already sheltered from all levels of taxation. Stick to funds which are normally taxable; these usually offer a higher rate of return. Also, look into zero coupon bonds (see Chapter 21) for funding your IRA.

How Should You Choose among These Investment Options?

One prime consideration should be how well you have otherwise provided for your retirement. If your IRA is your sole retirement plan, you should invest conservatively; if you have substantial savings outside of the IRA, income which you expect to continue after retirement, or a secure company pension plan, you can afford a bit more risk. Your age is another important factor. Here are some guidelines to use depending on your present age:

Age 20 to 40:   When you are young, growth should be your primary goal; a relatively high degree of risk is tolerable. Suggestion: Invest your IRA in a diversified portfolio of common stocks or in a mutual fund managed for growth of assets, not income.

Age 40 to 50:   Stocks are still an attractive choice. However, if you expect to begin withdrawing your IRA funds when you reach age $59\frac{1}{2}$, redirect some of your funds from growth stocks into current income-generating investments.

Age 50 to 60:   At this point, growth is less important, risk less acceptable. Move your investments out of stocks and into bonds, in order to minimize risk and increase your current flow of income.

Age 60 and over: By now, all your IRA funds should be in income-producing investments with maturities of 5 years and less. This will provide safety and maximum current interest.

What about Rollover Distributions to IRAs?

All eligible rollover distributions are subject to a mandatory 20 percent withholding tax. Although this 20 percent withholding would still be considered part of the distribution which is subject to income tax, you can claim a federal tax refund, if the 20 percent withholding results in overwithholding for the year. There are two ways to avoid current taxation on this mandatory 20 percent withholding.

1. You elect to do a "direct rollover." This means that your distribution is moved directly to another retirement plan or IRA rather than distributed to you. In the case of a direct rollover, the 20 percent withholding would not apply. Under this method, you would need to have your employer or plan coordinator write a check payable to the trustee of your new plan, putting on the memo line of the check the words "Direct Rollover." Once this transfer is made into your IRA, you can take the money out the very next day without the 20 percent withholding. However, you may do so only once a year. If you are under the age of 59½, the entire balance must be put back into an IRA within 60 days or a 10 percent penalty is imposed.

2. You may add your own after-tax funds, up to the amount withheld, to the amount that you actually received in order to roll over an amount equal to your entire taxable distribution. Sounds complicated? Use this as an example. Assume a participant elects to receive a lump-sum distribution of $100,000 from his or her retirement account. Because of the 20 percent withholding rule, the participant would receive only $80,000. However, since he or she is entitled to roll over the entire $100,000, $20,000 of personal funds could be added to bring the total amount of the rollover up to $100,000. The 20 percent withheld at the time of distribution would be refunded when the participant files his or her tax return. If the participant does not choose to add

the additional $20,000 personally but instead rolls over only $80,000 of the $100,000 received from the original trustee, he or she must include the $20,000 as taxable income for that year.

If there is a waiting period for you to get into your new employer's plan and you do not want to follow step 1 or 2 above, you can get the plan coordinator to transfer your funds to a "conduit" IRA. This type of IRA is used as a temporary account for rollovers in order to keep them separate from other IRA funds, since no commingling of funds is acceptable for rollovers. This conduit IRA must be set up at a place where no other IRA of yours exists.

The following points must be kept in mind when reviewing the 20 percent withholding:

1. The 20 percent withholding applies only to lump-sum withdrawals and not to periodic withdrawals such as retirees taking a monthly payout.

2. Two types of distributions are not eligible for rollovers and thus are not subject to the 20 percent withholding:

   ■ Required minimum distribution received after age $70\frac{1}{2}$

   ■ Payments received in 10 or more annual installments or in a series of equal installments extending over the participant's lifetime

3. It is the participant's responsibility to inform his or her employer or plan sponsor of a desire to transfer.

The IRA is certainly a plan to look into for your retirement, since it can become an excellent vehicle for future income. And on the topic of retirement plans, remember to plan for the future now because that is where you will be spending the rest of your life.

24

The 401(k), the SEP, and the KEOGH Plan

In two days, tomorrow will be yesterday.

An increasingly popular way of saving for retirement is the *401(k) plan*, named after the tax law provision that makes it possible. The 401(k) is known as the *deferred salary reduction plan* and allows an employee to set aside part of his or her salary into a tax-sheltered account that grows tax-free until after retirement. Don't confuse the 401(k) with a 403(b). A 403(b) is a retirement plan designed for employees of non-profit organizations (schools, hospitals, etc.), whereas the 401(k) is for employees of private, for-profit businesses. Salary deductions for a 403(b) are treated in the same manner as the funds in the 401(k) account, which is excluded from taxable income, while the interest earned compounds tax-deferred until you withdraw the funds.

How Does the 401(k) Differ from an Ordinary IRA?

Since you don't have to pay current income tax on the money you deposit in your 401(k) account, the plan is something like an individual retirement account. However, unlike an IRA, a 401(k) plan must be set up by your employer. In order to qualify, you must be a full-time employee over the age of 21 and working for the company at least 1 year. The annual limit for the 401(k) that you contribute yourself is 20 percent of your gross income or $9240 (1994), whichever is less. The amount you put into the fund is indexed to increase each year. In recent years this figure has averaged 3 percent annually. If there are matching funds from the employer, the maximum is the aggregate of 25 percent of total compensation up to $30,000. By contrast, an IRA has a limit of $2000 annually. Also, with an IRA you indicate the size of your contribution as a deduction on your federal income tax return. With a 401(k), this is not necessary. Your contribution is deducted from the income reported on your W-2 form, and therefore is automatically excluded from federal and state income taxes.

How Does the 401(k) Work?

The 401(k) is in actuality a profit-sharing plan with a cash or deferred arrangement (CODA). This CODA provision permits employees to contribute part of their salary to the 401(k) on a pretax basis, with the amount being deducted from their paychecks. The amount of compensation taken out of salary is not subject to federal, state, or local income tax but is subject to FICA (social security) tax. This money will grow in the account on a tax-deferred basis, as with most other qualified retirement plans.

At the time the 401(k) plan is established by the employer, a specific investment program is set up. The employer usually chooses an investment firm to manage the accounts, and a range of possible investment options is offered. These choices are usually more restricted than they would be with an IRA. Whereas almost any investment vehicle is permissible with an IRA, only a handful of options are allowed with a 401(k): a fixed-interest annuity, a mutual fund investing in stocks, a money market fund, and, perhaps, stock in the company itself. You can opt to put all your contributions into one or another investment vehicle, or you can split your contributions among two or more choices.

What about Withdrawal from a 401(k)?

If you leave the company, you can withdraw your 401(k) savings and keep the money if you wish. However, the amount becomes subject to income tax during that year. You can avoid taxation by rolling the money over into an IRA. To do so, you must transfer the money directly from your trustee to the IRA's trustee, making certain that you never take possession of the funds. In this trustee-to-trustee relationship, you will avoid the 20 percent withholding penalty that began in 1993. You are also eligible to withdraw your 401(k) money at any time without having to pay a penalty if you suffer a financial hardship.

Once you reach the age of 59½, the money in your 401(k) account is yours to do with as you please. Of course, it is taxable when you withdraw it. However, your income will probably be lower after you retire, and so might your tax bracket. And the 401(k) account has another major advantage over the IRA when withdrawal time comes. If you withdraw your IRA funds in a lump sum, you must suffer a big tax bite during that year. However, if you withdraw your 401(k) funds in a lump sum, you can use 5-year forward averaging to spread out and reduce the tax payments. (See Chapter 22.) This means that the withdrawal is taxed as if you'd received only one-fifth of the money each year for a period of 5 years. You may use 10-year forward averaging if you were born before 1936, but the tax rate table is different.

If the owner of the 401(k) dies before withdrawal, the amount of money in the plan is distributed to his or her beneficiaries, and the money is taxed as ordinary income to the beneficiaries. However, if the money is left to a surviving spouse, that spouse may transfer the funds to his or her IRA account.

As you can see, the 401(k) plan is a very attractive investment option for you as an employee, especially since the usual employer matching-contribution program in effect doubles your annual savings at no cost to you. More and more employers are offering 401(k) plans as part of their fringe-benefits packages and to supplement existing pension plans. In some regions, over half of all companies are currently offering or plan to offer 401(k) plans. If your employer is among those making this investment option available, take advantage of it. And if you can afford to contribute to both a 401(k) account and an IRA, do that, too. You'll benefit right now as well as when you retire.

How Does the SEP Work?

For a small business (proprietorship, partnership, corporation) the *simplified employee pension,* or *SEP,* is an excellent pension-planning tool, since it can help business owners, including those self-employed, to achieve financial security for their retirement. It was authorized in 1978 by Congress to give small businesses (even self-employed workers without employees) a program of current tax deduction and future pension benefits.

The business sets up an IRA for each employee and contributes, each year, as much as $22,500 or 15 percent (13.043 percent for self-employed) of earnings. These contributions are tax-deductible to the company. Employees may decide how to contribute the funds to their IRAs and can take the IRAs with them when they leave the firm. There is no complex administration, and the start-up and maintenance costs are slight. One of the major features of the SEP is the extra time allowed to initiate it. Many people look for last-minute tax deductions before the April 15 deadline. You can set up a SEP $3\frac{1}{2}$ months into the next year, as compared with the Keogh plan, which requires completion by the last day of the year.

What Should You Know about the SEP?

1. Employer contributions to the SEP are tax-deductible to the company and are not considered taxable income of the employee. These monies accumulate in the employee's SEP/IRA on a tax-deferred basis.

2. No start-up or annual filing costs are required to be sent to the U.S. Department of Labor. As its name implies, it is a simple plan to administer. The paperwork usually amounts to no more than a one-time completion of a model plan. Unless changes are made in the plan, you do not have to file annually, as you do with a Keogh.

3. All amounts from the SEP are considered ordinary income, with distribution of monies beginning no later than age 70½. Any withdrawal prior to age 59½ may be subject to a 10 percent penalty.

4. All eligible employees must be included in the plan. Eligibility is based on the employee (1) being 21 years of age or older, (2) earning at least $300 (plus inflation adjustment) per year, and (3) having worked for the business in 3 of the last 5 years.

5. The same percentage that the employer receives must be applied to each employee, including yourself.

6. Lump-sum distributions from the SEP do not qualify for special income averaging, as do Keogh plans.

7. Unlike conventional company pension plans, in which employees usually have to wait a number of years before gaining access to their contributions, the SEP allows employees immediate right to any contributions the employer makes for their benefit.

Has the Tax Reform Act Changed the SEP?

Under the TRA, a type of SEP known as *cash or deferred arrangement* (CODA) was created to permit each employee to make voluntary contributions (elective deferrals) to his or her own account. This contribution—15 percent of the employee's salary up to a maximum of $9240 (indexed) per year—is considered to be a pretax contribution and therefore is not counted for federal income tax purposes. However, the amount will count as a deduction for social security. The total of the employer and employee contributions cannot exceed the lesser of $22,500 or 15 percent of total compensation.

SEPs were created to develop retirement plans for small businesses and their employees as well as for self-employed individuals who have no employees. The plan is an attractive way to save for those future retirement years while saving currently on taxes.

How Does the Keogh Plan Work?

The Keogh plan is a pension plan designed for the self-employed individual, whether the work is full or part time. In other words, you can work for an employer full time, but if you have any income from self-employment, part of that self-employment income can be contributed to your own Keogh plan.

A Keogh plan account is similar to an IRA in several ways. Your annual contribution to a Keogh account reduces your taxable income, and the sums in your account grow tax-free until you withdraw your investment after reaching the age of $59\frac{1}{2}$; the upper limit on withdrawal is age $70\frac{1}{2}$. At that time, the sums you withdraw are treated as ordinary taxable income. However, your income will probably be lower after retirement, so that the size of your tax bite will be smaller. Early withdrawals prior to age $59\frac{1}{2}$ carry a 10 percent penalty. Therefore, as with an IRA, you should invest in a Keogh account only sums you don't expect to need until retirement. Liquidity is not one of the characteristics of a Keogh account.

What Are the Differences between the Keogh and the IRA?

As you will see subsequently, not everyone is eligible for a Keogh account. While the maximum amount you may contribute to an IRA in any year is $2000, you may invest up to a maximum of $30,000 or 25 percent of your earned income, whichever is less, in a Keogh account under the "money purchase" plan. This plan requires a fixed percentage of your income each year. If you have a "profit-sharing" Keogh, which allows varying contributions each year, the tax-deductible limit on contributions is 13.043 percent of your self-employment earnings, up to a maximum of $30,000.

Withdrawals from the two types of accounts are also handled differently. With both an IRA and a Keogh account, you can withdraw the money either in a lump sum upon retirement or in installments. However, if you withdraw your Keogh investment in a lump sum, you can take advantage of the 5-year forward averaging rule, which allows you to compute your taxable income as if the withdrawal had been spread out over a 5-year period. A 10-year forward averaging period is also available, subject to certain conditions (see Chapter 22). Thus the Keogh plan can produce significantly greater income tax savings at withdrawal time than the IRA.

How Do You Qualify for a Keogh Plan?

To qualify for a Keogh account, you must be self-employed as the sole proprietor of a business, an unincorporated professional, or a partner in any unincorporated partnership. In addition, if your business has any employees, you are required to include in the plan all those who have worked for you longer than 3 years. You must contribute to their retirement funds the same percentage of their salary that you are contributing to your own. (Naturally, the employer's share of the Keogh investment for employees is treated as a deductible business expense.) The Keogh funds may be invested in almost any kind of instrument favored by the employer, including a certificate of deposit, stocks and bonds, a money market fund, or an insurance account. Collectibles are virtually the only common type of investment not allowed. The employer may choose to manage the Keogh personally or may invest the money in an annuity contract purchased from an insurance company or a mutual fund managed by a broker.

Ever since their introduction, Keoghs have been among the most popular pension plans. In 1984, the contribution limits were raised from $15,000 or 15 percent of earned income to the present $30,000 or 25 percent indexed to inflation. This change has only increased the attractiveness of the Keogh plan. If you're eligible for a Keogh plan account, you should certainly give it serious consideration as an investment option. It is a kind of super IRA which allows the self-employed professional or business proprietor to reduce his or her current taxable income while saving a substantial sum toward retirement. And on the topic of planning, judge each day not by the harvest you reap, but by the seeds you plant.

25

Social Security

I don't mind being a senior citizen, I just
don't look forward to graduation.

Let's start from the beginning. Social security's retirement fund is not running out of money but is actually increasing each year. It is estimated that by the year 2000 the trust fund will have more than $4 trillion in assets, all invested in special U.S. government securities. So we will begin on this point.

People often overlook their social security benefits when calculating their projected retirement income. Financial planning is a system that must encompass all phases of investments, so know the rules of social security—because for many of us, it has become our most costly investment.

How Does the System Work?

As of 1994, both you and your employer contribute 6.2 percent of your wages to social security, up to a maximum of $60,600, and 1.45 percent to medicare with no limit. These contributions by both employees and employers are broken down into three separate trust funds:

OASI—old age and survivors insurance: This is a self-contained account separate from other U.S. Treasury revenue which will fully take care of benefit payments to retirees and their survivors. These funds may not be spent for any other purpose.

DI—disability insurance: The same rules apply here as to OASI except that benefit payments go for the disabled.

HI—health insurance :   Known also as Medicare, the fund pays all costs of hospital (Part A) but only 20 percent of doctor's fees and other charges (Part B). The balance is funded from general Treasury revenues.

You can qualify for social security retirement benefits in one of two ways:

1. As a worker by earning a minimal amount for at least 40 quarters.
2. As a nonworking spouse by being married to a retired or disabled worker. At retirement (age 65), the spouse will receive half of the benefit of the working spouse.

The working benefit you will receive is based on the 35 highest earning years, so if you began your career at 18 and retired at 65, the lowest 10 years of earnings will not count. This benefit, paid to you monthly,may be increased annually by the cost-of-living adjustment (COLA) based on the Consumer Price Index (CPI).

How Do Social Security Payments Work under the Tax Law?

Under the provisions of the 1984 Tax Reform Act, a formula was used to determine the degree to which social security benefits were subject to income tax. This formula set a "threshold income" (beginning with your adjusted gross income) below which benefits were not taxed. The threshold was $25,000 for single individuals and $32,000 for a married couple filing a joint return. Those whose income exceeded the threshold amount would be subject to income tax on up to one-half of their social security benefits.

In 1994, the new social security tax took hold. Whereas

prior to that date, 50 percent of the taxable portion of your social security could be taxed, the amount was raised to 85 percent in many cases. Under this tax law, you add half of your social security benefits to all other income (including tax-exempt income) in order to determine how much is subject to social security tax. If your total is under $25,000 (individual) or $32,000 (joint), then none of your social security is subject to tax. If, however the total is over this first threshold but under the new 1994 threshold of $34,000 and $44,000 respectively, then half of the excess income over the first threshold (up to a maximum of half of your social security) is taxable. If the total is over the second threshold of $34,000 or $44,000, then you must add 85 percent of that portion over the second threshold to a maximum of $4500 (individual) and $6000 (joint). Whichever figure is less, the maximum computation or 85 percent of your social security benefits, becomes taxable as social security income. Sound complicated? Here is an example.

Mr. And Mrs. Essex receive annual social security payments of $16,000. They also have adjusted gross income, as reported on their tax return, of $30,000 and receive nontaxable income from municipal bonds of $8000—for a total income of $38,000. Their computation for taxable social security income would be as follows:

1.	Income	$38,000
2.	Half of social security benefits	8,000
3.	Total income from all sources	46,000
4.	Excess of $44,000	2,000
5.	85% of line 4	1,700
6.	Maximum amount	6,000
7.	Add lines 5 and 6	7,700
8.	85% of your social security	13,600
9.	The lesser of line 7 or 8: your taxable social security income	7,700

A tax-saving tactic is to make a gift of tax-free investment instruments to your children. Municipal bonds are an example of instruments that can be used for this purpose. Your children, in turn, can return the interest payments to you in the form of a gift, which is not included in the social security computation. Of course, your children will then own the bonds. You must decide for yourself whether this is a reasonable option.

What Happens If You Want to Retire before Age 65?

Many individuals have asked me what I think about retiring before age 65. I have always felt that *it is better to retire too early than too late.* However, you have to understand the social security payout implications.

Consider retirement not as the goal of reaching retirement age, but as entering a retirement zone. At the center of this zone is the standard retirement age, which is 65 (if you were born before 1938) and 65 plus (up to a maximum of 67) if you were born after 1959. At that center point you will be entitled to receive 100 percent of your primary insurance amount (PIA) as it is computed from your record earnings. On the low side of the retirement zone is age 62, which will provide you with early retirement benefits between 70 percent and 80 percent of your PIA. It is 80 percent if your full retirement age is 65 and 70 percent if your full retirement age is 67. If you decide to work past age 65, you move to the other size of the zone, known as the *high end*. At this point you will receive a higher monthly social security benefit (more than 100 percent) when you do finally retire. The amount will range from a 3.5 percent increase to an 8 percent increase depending on your date of birth. At age 70, you will have reached the highest end of the retirement zone, and will not receive any further increase in benefits. However, you do not have to retire to collect your full social security check because you are entitled, at this age, to full benefits, no matter how much you earn.

Also, as far as social security benefits are concerned, it makes no difference what time of the year you retire. Most people in fact retire toward the end of a calendar year simply as a matter of convenience and personal preference. However, the social security law permits you to retire at any time during the year without forfeiting any benefits; payments start any month you choose, provided you meet all the conditions of eligibility. When you've set your retirement date, plan on applying for social security benefits about 3 months earlier. This leaves plenty of time to process your claim and handle any questions or problems that may arise.

How Do You Know You Are Getting Accurate Social Security Benefits?

It would be unthinkable for a person to let years go by without balancing a checkbook; yet that same individual will usually wait until age 65 before making certain that his or her social security account has been accurately credited. By then, if there are errors, it may be too late. However, there is a way to remedy this situation while you are presently employed. Contact your social security office and ask for the free "Request for Earnings and Benefit Estimate" statement, which will verify your earnings record to date. Merely save your W-2s and compare the figures. Forty quarters of coverage will entitle you to receive full social security benefits at retirement. By periodically examining your social security account (every 3 years), you will be assured that the income paid from your account will represent all that you have earned.

Are There Any Penalties If You Work Part Time after You Retire?

Retirees who go back to work are subject to a most unpopular law known as the Retirement Earnings Test. This rule penalizes those who reenter the work force after they begin to collect social security. Congress, however, is already committed to taking one small step toward reducing the penalties on the working elderly. It has raised the limitations in 1994 on earnings of those between the ages of 65 and 69 to $11,160 and cut the penalty on earnings over this ceiling to 33 percent. Between the ages of 62 and 65, the dollar amount is lowered to $8040 and the penalty increased to 50 percent. Once you reach age 70, you can collect full benefits, regardless of the amount of your earnings.

When social security was first set up during the Depression, one purpose was to push older workers out of the labor force to make room for unemployed younger people. That may not be desirable in the mid-1990s. And it may not be affordable after that. A move is under way in Congress to abolish completely the earnings penalty on seniors who are 65 or older. A single bill can't solve the complex problems of social security or create a happy balance among generational interests. However, it could begin to free people financially to experiment with new solutions and to lead more productive lives after age 65.

Are There Special Rules for Women on Social Security?

Because women live longer than men (usually about 7 years), they are more dependent on the government for retirement benefits. Also, women are penalized more than men if they keep working while receiving social security benefits. Thus it is of major importance to understand the role of the female and social security. The age regulations are the same for everyone. As mentioned previously, you can get full retirement benefits at age 65 if you were born before 1938. The age of full retirement rises slowly until age 67 if you were born in 1960 or later. If you are a widow or a divorced widow, you can begin drawing checks as early as age 62, but at only 80 percent (70 percent when the new law of age 67 is fully phased in) of what you would have received at age 65. When you are ready for retirement, you will have the following options:

1. Income based on your own work record
2. Income based on your spouse's work record
3. Income based on your divorced spouse's benefits
4. Income based on divorced widow's benefits
5. Income based on widow's benefits

It is interesting to note that widows and divorced widows who qualify both on their own work records and as widows can enjoy the benefits of both. They can receive reduced benefits at age 62, based on their own work record, and at age 65 they can choose to begin receiving a full widow's benefit.

What Are the Family Benefits of a Social Security Plan?

The social security tax that you and your employer pay places you and your family in line for collecting more than just retirement benefits. You may also collect Medicare and disability income. If you become disabled, you get benefits at any age (assuming you have enough quarters of coverage). In order to qualify for disability benefits, you must have earned 20 credits of coverage during the 10-year period ending with the calendar quarter you became disabled. However, if your disability is blindness or if you become disabled before reaching age 31, more lenient rules apply.

A child (either natural or adopted) may be entitled to benefits upon the death of a parent. To qualify, the child must have been a dependent and (1) be unmarried and either under age 18 or, if a full-time high school student, under age 19, or (2) regardless of age, be disabled before age 22. The child then would receive a monthly benefit equal to 50 percent of the amount the parent would have gotten at age 65.

Bear in mind that there is a maximum on family benefits. The benefit percentages for family members are the maximum each relative can collect. When more than one family member is collecting benefits based on the insured's earnings record, the actual size of their benefits checks is likely to be smaller. Why? The social security law places a dollar cap on the total monthly benefits paid to a family based on the earnings of one family member.

Thus, you can see that in order to plan for retirement, all areas of income, whether actual or potential, must be considered. And on the topic of planning for retirement, remember that the time to fix the roof is when the sun is shining.

26
Will It?

The only real thing of value we can give our
children is what we are, not what we have.

This chapter is essential because of all the possible threats to your family's assets (inflation, downturn in the market, etc.) only one is definite, and that is your death. I have discussed, in previous chapters, topics ranging from financial planning for young children through financial planning for retirement. Now this chapter completes the life cycle.

By law you have the right to own property, to use it as you wish during your lifetime, and to determine who shall receive it after you die. Everyone makes use of the first two rights, but many give up their third-party right by failing to write a will. Did you know that 7 out of 10 Americans die without a will? This is a shame, because without one you lose control of your estate. This loss affects not only what happens to what you own but also the people who should receive your property after you die. Writing a will is a way of taking care of the people you love in a time period when you will not be there.

What Is a Will?

A *will* is simply a set of written instructions as to what should be done with your property after you die. The *testator* (the person whose will it is) and the lawyer will both make important decisions today that will take place in the future and affect other people's lives. A will names those people who will receive your property in the amounts you decide. It also assigns specific shares of your property to each one, and describes any particular conditions under which the distribution should occur. Remember, this must be in writing and witnessed. If there are verbal commitments by the testator regarding the distribution of his or her estate upon death, these oral expressions will have no legal basis when the testator dies.

If you fail to prepare a properly executed will, several unpleasant consequences may follow: Your property may not be distributed as you had hoped it would be, your heirs may suffer a greater tax burden and higher administrative costs, and your family and friends may be subject to needless worry and squabbling. Preparing a will is an essential part of meeting your financial responsibilities. An improperly drawn-up or executed will can be rejected by the courts. The decision can render the document invalid, leaving your estate without a will (intestate)—a topic covered at the end of this chapter.

How Do You Begin to Draw Up a Will?

Before you consider who should receive your possessions at death, you must have some idea of what you own. Start by listing all your assets with their real or estimated value. The total is your gross estate. Because state and federal estate taxes can cut into your gross estate, it's important to know the exact value of your assets. If your taxable estate (equal to your gross estate less debts and expenses) exceeds $600,000, your survivors will face federal estate taxes— which can be steep. No federal tax is due, however, on the first $600,000 of value due (the unified tax credit). Presently (1994) there is serious discussion about bringing down the $600,000 exemption to only $200,000. However, nothing has been finalized. It should also be noted that no federal estate tax is due on assets left to your spouse or to a charity. The law, however, varies from state to state on the treatment of estate tax.

Because personal and family circumstances change, you should review your will at least once every 5 years to make certain that it still reflects your current wishes and needs. You should consider a change in your will when one or more of the following events occur:

If you marry, separate, or divorce

If your beneficiary or executor dies

If you move to another state

If federal, state, or estate laws change

If family circumstances change

If financial matters change

If you change your mind

If only minor changes are needed from time to time, these can be made by means of a written statement (called a *codicil*) attached to the original document. The help of a lawyer is needed for amending a will.

As the years go by, we all accumulate assets that are impossible to list in the will. You cannot keep amending the document every time you purchase something of value. Thus you will need a provision in your will, known as a *residuary clause,* that describes how the remainder of your assets not listed in the will should be distributed.

Who Carries Out the Instructions in a Will?

The instructions you leave in your will are to be carried out by a person you designate as the *executor.* If no one is named in the will as executor (or "personal representative," as in Florida and some other states), the court will appoint an administrator. The job of executor is an important, sometimes burdensome one, and may include any or all of the following duties:

1. The executor must obtain the original copy of the will and submit it to probate—that is, request court approval of its validity.

2. The executor may be required to publish a notice of death for a specified period of time.

3. The executor must inventory, appraise, and safeguard all assets of the estate.

4. The executor must open a checking account on behalf of the estate and maintain complete records of all transactions.

5. The executor must apply for all appropriate death benefits, including those available through social security, pension plans, the Veterans Administration, labor unions, and fraternal organizations.

6. The executor must pay all outstanding debts of the deceased.

7. The executor must file and pay local, state, federal income, and estate taxes.

8. The executor must distribute all remaining assets according to the terms of the will.

9. The executor may be required to submit a final accounting to the court.

As you see, it's necessary to choose wisely when naming an executor, so it's best to make certain that the person you have in mind is willing to undertake the job and understands what it entails. I have always recommended that a spouse or adult child, a close friend, or a relative be chosen over a lawyer. The major reason is, of course, cost.

It is just as important for a wife to have a will as for her husband. A married couple often have interlocking or reciprocal wills prepared at the same time. These are separate documents that are carefully interrelated and designed to meet the mutual objectives of both parties. For example, his-and-her wills should specify how the children are to be cared for in the event both parents die at the same time. And on the topic of marriage, how you own your money is just as important as knowing what you own. Transferring assets from one spouse to another might in some cases be your best financial move. For instance, a joint savings or checking account could be convenient today, but the surviving spouse might need those funds if the account is "frozen" when one of the account holders dies. Also, the law will protect the rights of spouses to receive a minimum share of an estate. In other words in most states spouses cannot be completely written out of the will unless a prenuptial agreement states so. Also, a child who is not mentioned in the will may be entitled to a portion of his or her legal share as if there were no will available. However, this does not preclude a parent from excluding a child if specific mention is made in the will.

How Can You Be Certain That the Distribution of the Estate Will Be without Problems?

You can make probate (the settling of the will) easier by following these simple procedures:

1. If you have made previous wills, tell your lawyer to destroy all earlier ones.

2. Choose a successor executor if your original choice cannot serve. Also, list contingent beneficiaries in the event your first choice may die before you or decline the inheritance.

3. In the event you have young children, pick a guardian in case they should become orphans.

4. Devise an order of payment if your estate becomes too small to pay all legacies.

5. Decide in advance whether the executor is to receive the standard compensation or a bequest from you.

6. Keep your will in a safe place (your lawyer's office and a copy at home) but preferably not in a safe deposit box; if the box is sealed upon your death, getting into it may be time-consuming and difficult. If you insist on the safe

deposit box, open two of them and put your will in your spouse's safe deposit box and vice versa.

7. When making any bequest, leave a percentage of your estate rather than a fixed dollar amount, because your assets may either grow or shrink over the years. For example, it is better to say that "I leave 10 percent of my estate to XYZ Charity" than to give a specific amount— $50,000, for example. If your estate should be reduced in value for whatever reason by the time you pass on, the $50,000 could be excessive in relation to the needs of those to whom you are leaving the balance of the money. Just remember that you will not be able to bequeath any property you own that is jointly held.

8. Make certain that your will is properly drafted or it may be interpreted in a manner that you did not wish. For example, if you want to disinherit a child, be sure to specify in your will that you are doing it. If not, the child might later claim to have been overlooked by mistake. Don't use your will to throw your final insult at any individual; find some other means to "get even." Also bear this thought in mind. As soon as someone named as beneficiary in your will (including your spouse) enters a nursing facility, make certain that the person's name is immediately taken out of your will. Otherwise, upon your death the property left to that beneficiary can be seized in order to pay the nursing home costs.

9. In certain situations, it's better to leave property in trusts rather than in outright bequests. A trust is simply an arrangement for transferring your title to your property (your ownership) to another person or company to hold in trust for you or anyone you designate. Trusts set up under a will are called *testamentary trusts* and become effective upon the death of the person who drew up the will. The trustee holds the property you otherwise would have bequeathed outright, and invests and administers it for the benefit of your stated beneficiaries. Trusts are frequently written into wills to ease the impact of estate

taxes (particularly if a great deal of money is involved and to protect the interests of minors until they have matured). There are countless ways of setting up trusts, so great care must be exercised to obtain the best possible legal tax advantages. (See Chapter 27.)

Bear in mind that not all property goes through the courts (probate). Any asset that has a designated beneficiary would pass outside of the will. In fact, a large portion of your estate is likely to pass outside probate court without any effort on your part. For example, the balance of your employee retirement plan, IRA, or Keogh account, as well as the proceeds of your life insurance policy, will go directly to your designated beneficiaries. Also, any property you own jointly with rights of survivorship will automatically go to the co-owner upon your death. If you live in one of the community-property states (Arizona, California, Idaho, Louisiana, Nevada, Texas, and Washington), half of all the assets that you acquired during your marriage (except gifts or inheritances) belong to your spouse, with the other half passing under your will.

How Can Assets Be Owned?

In order for you to plan financially, you must understand the concept of ownership. Joint ownership is the most common method by which married couples take title to their house and other assets. It may also be used by others who wish to share the control of some property. Let's examine the three basic types of joint ownership, each of which has certain special legal and financial characteristics you should know about.

1. *Joint tenancy:* With this type of ownership, both owners have a complete and undivided interest in the property. When one owner dies, the property immediately passes to the surviving owner without having to go to probate. For joint tenancy to be in effect, the names of both owners must appear on the deed or other ownership document.

Both married couples and single people use joint tenancy as a method of guaranteeing ease of transfer of property upon death of one of the owners. However, it can't be considered a substitute for a will. As an illustration, joint tenancy may not automatically produce the desired result after death. Suppose you and your sister buy a summer home together, taking title as joint tenants. You die first, and your sister dies shortly thereafter. Upon your death, your share in the summer home passes immediately to your sister. Therefore, when she dies, the home goes entirely to her heirs; your own heirs will receive no share in it. This may or may not be what you intended.

2. *Tenancy in common:*   With tenancy in common, each owner has title to half the property. If one owner dies, his or her share does not automatically pass to the survivor. Instead, it is disposed of in accordance with the will of the deceased. This method is used by friends or relatives who wish to form a joint ownership and share in its benefits while they are alive but want to retain the right to decide individually what happens to their share of the property when they die.

3. *Community property:*   In Arizona, California, Idaho, Louisiana, Nevada, Texas, and Washington, husband and wife share equally in any property either one accumulates while they are living together. This is so regardless of whose name appears on the deed or ownership papers. Such jointly owned property is called community property, and the states where this is a matter of law are called community-property states.

There are exceptions under the law to community property: (1) property obtained by either spouse prior to the marriage; (2) property acquired after marriage by gift or inheritance; and (3) property acquired in non-community-property states. Note that the fact that you have moved from a community-property state to a non-community-property state does not automatically exempt you and your spouse from the community property law. You are still subject to the law for property you obtained while married and a resident of the community-property state.

What Happens If You Die without a Will?

If there is no will whatsoever, severe problems can arise. Without a will (*intestate*) you, in essence, have condemned your estate to an unnecessarily prolonged and expensive wait. What happens is that your local court appoints an individual who will administer the distribution of your property in accordance with the laws of your state. However, with a will, it becomes your decision—not that of an outside administrator—as to what will happen to your estate.

States vary in the handling of after-death distributions of property intestate. In some states, the surviving spouse will receive the property if there are no descendants. In other states, parents may be involved in the distribution. In some states, if there are descendants, the spouse will receive one-third of the property, and the children will get equal shares of the balance. If there is only one child, the spouse will receive half. If there are children of a deceased child, they will share in the same manner of their deceased parent. If there is no spouse or child, the mother and father of the deceased will each get one-half of the estate. If there is only one parent, the survivor will get all. If both parents are deceased, brothers or sisters will share equally; and if they are dead, their children will receive the parent's share. If no brothers or sisters exist, the estate will be distributed to more distant relatives in patterns which vary from state to state. If there are no surviving relatives, the estate will go to the state by *escheat*.

Remember that making a will is one of the wisest investments of your life—and after. And on the thought of planning, it is not what happens to you that counts. It is what you do with what happens to you that is important.

27
Trust Me

*This is not the end, nor is it even the
beginning of the end. This is just the end of
the beginning.*

Are There Alternatives to Having a Will?

A will and a trust are both legal documents that transfer
your assets to your designated heirs upon your death. A
will names an executor and a trust names a trustee to distribute those assets. But that's where the similarity ends.

One of the major drawbacks of a will is the cost and time
to probate it. The process, at a minimum, can take 4 to 8
months, and if you have property in another state, or if any
disgruntled relatives contest the will, your heirs might have
to wait for years for the settlement. Also, administrative and
legal costs during the probate process could run 5 percent
or more of the estate. The easiest way to avoid probate and
have your assets transferred immediately is to set up a *revocable* or living trust (*intervivos trust*), which transfers your
assets to the trust while you are alive. A living trust must
not be confused with a living will, which is a document in
which you express your wish to give up extraordinary medical treatment if you should become terminally ill.

Since the use of trusts in financial planning is extremely
complex, a full discussion of trusts is not the purpose of this
chapter. Rather, I have provided a brief description of the
many uses of trusts and their impact on financial planning.

It is my intent to encourage you to continue to explore with your attorney, and any other person involved in finance, the many aspects of trusts that may meet your specific needs.

How Do You Create a Revocable Living Trust?

A living trust is created to be effective during the lifetime of the one who creates the trust. It is revocable if the creator states in the trust agreement that he or she has the right during his or her lifetime to terminate (revoke) or change the conditions of the trust at any time and without the permission of anyone else. A living trust may be irrevocable if the creator does not reserve the right to revoke the trust.

When creating the living trust, you must realize that you are required to switch the titles of everything you are placing in the trust from your name to the name of the trust. In every trust document, there are three principals. First, there is the *trustor* (or grantor), who is the person or persons who created the trust and transferred the assets into it. Second, there is the *trustee*, who is the person or persons charged with the task of managing the assets in the trust. He or she makes all the financial and business decisions concerning the trust assets and has the right to buy, sell, trade, exchange, mortgage, and encumber. In fact, the trustee can do virtually anything with the trust assets except use them for his or her own benefit. These rights are reserved for the *beneficiary*, whose only role is to enjoy the assets.

When you create your trust, you can lawfully become (in most states) all three parties: the trustor, the trustee, and the beneficiary. Under this arrangement, you can act as your own trustee, giving yourself control over your estate while you are alive. You then can appoint a successor trustee if you should become incapacitated or should die. Because the trust is revocable, it can be changed at any time you wish.

What Are the Major Advantages of the Revocable Living Trust?

In addition to avoiding the costs of probate, a living trust affords many advantages to both the trustor and his or her heirs.

1. A revocable trust can be changed or terminated at any time before the trustor dies.

2. Because the trustor retains the right to get back all property transferred to a revocable trust, those assets are not considered gifts for estate, gift, or income tax purposes. Any income that comes from the assets in the trust will remain taxable to the trustor during his or her lifetime.

3. Unlike a will, a living trust can (in many states) attempt to shield the estate from creditors. With a will, the executor is required to notify the creditors of the death of the maker of the will—by mail and newspaper advertisement—so that they can submit any claims against the estate. No such publicity would take place in a living trust, since no public notification would be needed. Thus many people believe that once assets have been transferred to a living trust, they cannot be accessed by creditors. This is not generally true. Most states have laws that allow creditors to get back what is owed to them from the assets of such trusts.

4. The trust avoids the courts and the general public. For example, when an estate goes through probate, the court freezes its assets for several months and makes notice that interested parties can come forward if they wish to contest the will. However, the assets of the trust are not frozen, and in many cases the trust is dissolved and assets distributed to the beneficiaries long before the disgruntled heir has a chance to act. He or she would then have to sue each beneficiary separately.

5. A living trust provides for the designation of future heirs. For example, if you decide to leave all your worth

to your son Tom and years after your death your son should get divorced (or die), Tom's wife will wind up with most, if not all, of your assets. If she should remarry and begin a new family, your son's children (your grandchildren) could wind up receiving little or none of the inheritance that you left their father, Tom—funds you had assumed would be later used for their benefit. A living trust could keep your assets intact so that they would not be distributed to your son upon your death. This method can be used to ensure your grandchildren the rightful access to your funds regardless of what happens to your son or to his marriage. The procedure is simple. You name Tom your successor trustee and set up the trust so that he will be able to draw income and a small portion of the principal while he lives. At his death or divorce, or at a certain period of time you designate (when the children reach age 21, 30, 40, or whatever you determine), the trust would be terminated and the assets given to Tom's children (your grandchildren). The wife would have no control in this situation.

Here is another example. Suppose this is your second marriage, and a good one, but you want to leave your assets to your children from your previous marriage. You may think that your wishes would be followed in a will, but that may not be the case. In many states, the law says that you cannot disinherit a spouse. Thus, even though you decided to leave all your property to your children, there could develop a successful challenge in the courts resulting in the possible loss of a portion of your estate against your wishes. With a living trust (in some states), the property in the trust that passes to the children at your death cannot be challenged by a surviving spouse.

6. Although not generally known, anyone owning real estate in more than one state should have a living trust. This is so because the trust will avoid "ancillary probate," a costly, time-consuming judicial process that develops when death occurs to the owner of real estate property in a state other than the one that the deceased owner lived

in. Also, a living trust can be a source of comfort if you should become incapacitated. If a successor trustee is appointed, a debilitating illness will not cause financial hardship, since your trustee has the authority to pay your bills and handle your investments in a prudent manner. It thus avoids the possibility of having guardianship proceedings, which are costly and difficult to administer. Another simple method to accomplish the same objective is to designate a durable "power of attorney" to someone to make financial and living decisions on your behalf in the event you should become incapacitated.

What Are the Disadvantages of the Living Trust?

Although you do not have to go through the costly process of probate, the living trust is not without disadvantages.

1. By creating it, you have to place everything you own into the trust. If you hold any assets outside the trust, you may have to go through probate anyway. You can remedy this drawback by placing any "outside assets" into joint ownership with right of survivorship. Bear in mind that jointly held property can duplicate much the same benefits as a living trust, since the property will pass outside the courts (probate) and will go directly to the surviving joint owner.

2. It will almost always cost more to establish a living trust than a will. Legal fees can be higher and assets must actually be transferred to the trust, which can add additional costs. Also, if you appoint another person as trustee, you will have to pay a fee in accordance with state law (unless the trustee waives the fee).

3. The right to choose your own fiscal year to defer taxes will be lost.

4. The funds in the trust must be used up before the trustor can get any social service benefits (Medicaid, for example).

5. No tax advantage regarding estate taxes is gained by the revocable trust. Nor is there any income tax savings, since all income from the trust passes through to the individual's personal income tax return.

6. You may need to have a simple will regardless of the living trust because you cannot use a trust to name a guardian for your minor children.

7. You will need a will with a "pour-over" clause stating that any property that you forgot to put into your living trust should go there after your death. Those assets will then be subject to probate, but it will not be a lengthy or costly process if your estate is small ($500 in New Hampshire to $60,000 in California) and if the majority of your assets lie within the confines of the living trust. This extra process may take only a few days to complete. Yet it is crucial to have such a pour-over clause, since there most certainly could be assets that you overlooked while making the living trust.

8. Certain types of assets, such as jewelry and automobiles, are difficult to place in a trust because insurance companies are often reluctant to write a policy for a trust. Also, some assets need not be placed in a trust because they already pass (upon death) to the named beneficiary outside of the probate court. These assets could include IRAs, retirement benefits, life insurance proceeds, and annuities. Finally, under certain circumstances a living trust could be rendered inoperative and probate would be required. This situation might arise when:

   ■ Assets are currently subject to litigation (in the event of a lawsuit)
   ■ A tax audit is in progress

What Other Vehicles Are Available for Estate Planning?

If you were to die tomorrow, the odds are that your heirs would be able to settle your estate without paying an inheritance tax because of changes in federal and state tax codes in the past two decades. The federal exemption was only $60,000 in 1976 but is $600,000 in 1994. However, there are some members of Congress who advocate financing the cost of any new long-term health plan with a reduction of the $600,000 estate tax exemption down to $200,000. Nevertheless, until that day occurs, the federal tax is based on your taxable estate and the taxable portion of any gifts you made during your life. Adding taxable gifts to an estate is a way for the government to discourage people from dodging the federal estate tax by giving away all their property before they die. You can give up to $10,000 each year to as many people as you wish tax-free, and if your spouse joins in making the gift, $20,000 per recipient tax-free is permitted. Any amount over this annual exclusion is taxable.

If you give more than $10,000 to a couple, you can avoid any IRS hassle if you make out two separate checks. For example, a $20,000 gift to your son and his wife should be written in two checks of $10,000 each, one to your son and one to his wife. If you wish to give a sizable amount at one time, you can do so through self-cancellation installment notes (SCIN), which will cancel out over a period of years. For example, you loan $50,000 to your son, accepting five annual notes of $10,000 each. As agreed, one note is to be paid back to you each year. But at the anniversary of each note, you forgive its payment, thus meeting the requirement of the $10,000 gift limit. However, if you should die during the period that the notes are still outstanding, the value of the notes will remain in your estate and will be considered for estate tax purposes.

For those of you who have sizable estates, there is a method of leaving large funds without heavy federal taxation. By bequeathing the estate to your spouse, no tax is incurred. When the surviving spouse dies, tax is then applied to the beneficiaries of the estate over $600,000. However, by creating a bypass trust, you arrange to have up to $1,200,000 passed onto your children tax-free. Here's how it works. In your will you place up to $600,000 in a bypass trust and leave the rest to your spouse. In this way, the lifetime exemption ($600,000) and the unlimited marital deduction that is allowed shield the estate from federal estate taxes. The bypass trust pays income to your spouse and names the children as beneficiaries when the spouse dies. No control can be exercised by the spouse over the bypass trust. When the spouse does pass on, the amount of the trust is not part of his or her estate and so can be passed along (coupled with the spouse's estate up to $600,000) tax-free. Since no one can predict who will die first, both spouse's should provide for this trust.

How Does an Irrevocable Trust Work?

The word *irrevocable* has been bantered around as a way of sheltering assets from nursing-home seizure. All too often I encounter situations in which older people (especially widows) are so concerned about the high cost of nursing facilities that they contemplate placing their assets, through an irrevocable trust, into the hands of their children. Robert Browning wrote "Grow old along with me, the best is yet to be." That statement may not be true for seniors, since the best years may have already passed. No matter what any poet, orator, or sage may say, old age is still old age. Someone once said that you know you are growing older when everything hurts and what doesn't hurt doesn't work. Older people are of interest to doctors and hospitals, real estate brokers, and travel agents, not always as people, but as sources of income. As your ability to earn money decreases, so too does your stature as a person. Therefore, keep that money for yourself, having the knowledge that you are financially independent. Eliminate this aspect of your life by depositing your funds into the hands of your children through an irrevocable trust and you will quickly learn that the parent-child relationship can reverse itself. Remember that a parent should never have to ask in the future for any money given in the past.

Also, effective on August 11, 1993, the laws governing

Medicaid were changed. "Medicaid planning," as some call it, is a set of loopholes that allow older people with means to avoid the cost of nursing homes. Through various methods, these people give most of their assets to their heirs, thus making themselves eligible for government assistance. Under new rulings these gifts (set up as irrevocable trusts) must be given away at least 36 months (in some cases up to 60 months if assets are transferred to a trust rather than to a person) before Medicaid takes effect.

Aside from that point, the irrevocable trust does serve a purpose in financial planning for a large estate. This type of trust cannot be changed once it is written; thus the name *irrevocable*. As you are aware, estates over $600,000 are levied with estate taxes when the assets of the deceased are distributed to the heirs. These taxes must be paid within 9 months after death. However, the taxes can be reduced by the irrevocable trust if the maker is willing to give away certain assets before he or she dies.

If you leave more than $600,000, almost everything (with few exceptions) above that figure will be subject to federal estate tax. This is the point at which the irrevocable living trust comes into play. Assume that you have a $300,000 term life insurance policy. This insurance policy means nothing to you now but at your death it will add $300,000 to your estate. If your present estate is worth $500,000, your heirs will receive less money from your estate simply because the insurance policy proceeds will be counted as part of your assets, putting the total over the $600,000 exemption. To avoid the estate tax on the additional $200,000 ($800,000 − $600,000) you can set up an irrevocable trust that contains only the insurance policy. A trustee is named (other than yourself or your spouse so the asset is not in either of your estates) and that trustee becomes the owner (also perhaps the beneficiary) of the policy. The trustee pays the insurance premium that you gift into the trust. As long as the policy has been placed into the trust at least 3 years before your death, none of the $200,000 benefits will be counted as part of the $600,000 exemption.

It is obvious that any trust should be set up by an estate attorney sensitive to your needs. Interview several lawyers and tell each one as much as you can about your estate. You may lack the legal knowledge but certainly you can evaluate how comfortable you feel discussing family and financial matters with each attorney. And on the topic of trusts, get everything done before you are.

Epilogue

I hope that your reading of the material in this book has given you insight into the financial world and has taken the "utterly confused" status of investing into a more comprehensible realm. Bear in mind:

To look is one thing.

To see what you look at is another.

To understand what you see is a third.

To learn from what you understand is something else.

But to act on what you learn is all that really matters.

And that is the point. You must act now so that you can build a firm financial future for you and your family. Remember that the flowers of all tomorrows are in the seeds of today.

Glossary

adjustable-rate mortgage: A type of mortgage in which the interest rate charged may be changed at fixed intervals, usually in response to changes in some predetermined financial index.

amortize: To spread the cost over a period of time.

annuity: A form of insurance in which the policyholder, called the *annuitant,* pays a specified sum of money and in return receives regular payments for the rest of his or her life.

appreciation: An increase in the value of any property; used especially in reference to an increase in the value of a stock, bond, or other security.

assay: To analyze gold or silver bullion and so determine the proportion of precious metal it contains.

back-end load: A sales fee or commission charged by the management of a mutual fund at the time the shares in the fund are sold. (*See also* front-end load.)

balloon mortgage: A type of mortgage in which the entire principal comes due within 2 to 5 years, at which time the loan must be repaid or refinanced at current interest rates.

banker's acceptance: A negotiable time draft (known as BA) used in international trade. It is also used as a safe short-term investment in the money market. It usually matures in 90 days and is guaranteed to be paid at maturity by the bank.

beneficiary: The person who receives financial benefit as a result of a will, an insurance policy, or a trust fund.

bond: An IOU issued by a corporation or government agency promising to pay a specified amount of interest for a specified period of time in exchange for an amount of money being lent to the corporation or agency.

broker: A person or firm engaged in buying or selling stocks, bonds, real estate, or other investment instruments on behalf of another person or firm. Brokers are normally licensed by one or more government agencies that monitor and regulate their activities.

bullion: Gold or silver of a specified purity, in the form of coins or, more commonly, bars or ingots.

bypass trust: A trust allowing the surviving spouse of the trustor to receive income from the property during the spouse's lifetime, after which the property passes to the designated heirs.

callable bond: A bond which may be redeemed at the option of the issuing corporation or government agency before its maturity date.

capital: The total assets of a firm, including cash, land, buildings, equipment, investments, and accounts receivable.

capital gains: Profits from the sale of securities or real estate. Under the Tax Reform Act of 1986, there is no longer any difference in the designation of long-term capital gain and short-term capital gain, as all gains are now treated the same. Prior to 1987, a long-term gain (held for more than 6 months) would receive favorable income tax treatment. All capital gains are currently (1994) taxed at a maximum of 28 percent.

cash value: *See* surrender value.

certificate of deposit: A certificate representing an investment of a specified sum of money in a bank at a specified interest rate guaranteed for a particular period of time.

closing costs: Costs paid by the buyer of a home at the time of purchase. Closing costs include such charges as appraisal and surveying fees, title search costs, and lawyers' fees, and range from 2 to 10 percent of the purchase price of the home.

collateral: Property whose value is offered as a guarantee of repayment of a loan. If the loan is not repaid, the creditor is entitled to ownership of the collateral.

commercial bank: A bank which primarily serves business firms, although most commercial banks also accept deposits from and make loans to individuals.

common stock: A security that represents partial ownership in the issuing corporation. The holder of a share of common stock has the right to receive part of the company's earnings and to vote on certain policy decisions facing the company. (*See also* preferred stock.)

compound interest: Interest computed by applying the percentage rate not only to the principal but also to previously earned interest. The more frequently interest is compounded, the greater the effective yield of an investment.

condominium: A form of real estate ownership in which the owner holds the title to his or her own dwelling unit as well as a share in common properties such as lobbies, parking areas, and recreational facilities.

convertible bond: A corporate bond which may be exchanged at the option of the bondholder for shares of common stock in the same corporation.

cooperative: A form of real estate in which the owner buys one or more shares in a corporation that owns and manages land and buildings. Each share in the corporation entitles its owner to occupy part of the property, such as an apartment.

coupon bond: A bond with interest coupons attached that are clipped by the holder and redeemed at specified intervals for interest payments.

credit union: A savings institution that is owned by its depositors, who are technically considered shareholders. Like a savings bank, a credit union accepts deposits and makes loans, often at lower interest rates than those offered by banks.

creditor: A person or institution to which a debt is owed. The holder of a bond issued by a corporation, for example, is a creditor of the corporation.

custodial account: A savings or investment account, often in the name of a child, with another person, such as a parent, listed as custodian. The custodian manages the account, but the income belongs to the owner of the account and may normally be used only for his or her benefit.

debenture: A corporate bond whose value is not guaranteed by a pledge of collateral.

depreciation: A decline in the value of a piece of property over time. The depreciation of income-producing property is treated as a loss and so is deductible from income for income tax purposes; the amount of the tax deduction is computed by formulas that vary according to the nature of the property.

diversification: Investment of funds in a variety of instruments having differing yields, maturities, and degrees of risk. Diversification is generally considered a beneficial investment strategy.

dividend: A portion of a company's profits distributed to the stockholders. In a given year, a company's board of directors may or may not pay a dividend, depending on the company's financial status and anticipated future needs.

dividend reinvestment policy (DRIP): The automatic reinvestment back into the company of dividends earned on corporate securities for future earnings to the investor. Usually there is no commission charge for the service.

down payment: A partial payment for a piece of property, such as a home, made at the time of purchase, with the understanding that the balance will be paid later.

equity: The value of a piece of property to its owner over and above any portion of that value which has been offered as collateral for a loan. For example, the owner of a house worth $150,000 on which a $90,000 mortgage has been taken has $60,000 in equity.

executor: A person named in a will to manage the settlement of the estate according to the instructions given in the will.

401(k): Known as the deferred salary reduction plan, it allows an employee to set aside part of his or her salary (maximum $8994 or 20 percent of earnings) into a tax-sheltered account which grows tax-free until withdrawal.

face value: The value of a stock, bond, or insurance policy, usually printed on the front (or "face") of the document. The face value of a security usually differs from its selling price.

Federal Reserve: The central monetary authority of the United States. The Federal Reserve issues currency, sells U.S. government securities, and extends credit to member banks.

foreclosure: The process whereby the holder of a mortgage receives ownership of a property after the owner has failed to repay the loan.

front-end load: A sales fee or commission charged by the management of a mutual fund at the time the shares in the fund are purchased. (*See also* back-end load.)

income averaging: A method of computing income tax liability by which an unusually large amount of income received in a single year is spread out over several years, thus reducing the rate of taxation.

individual retirement account (IRA): A savings or investment plan which allows an individual to accumulate funds toward retirement while deferring income taxes on both the amount invested and the interest earned.

inflation: an increase in the general level of prices for goods and services in an economy.

insurance: A contract in which one party—usually a company organized for the purpose—promises to pay a specified sum of money in the event that the second party suffers a financial loss through death, accident, injury, or some other misfortune.

intestacy: The condition of dying without having made a valid will. When a person dies intestate, his or her estate is usually distributed in accordance with state laws.

junk bond: A corporate bond rated BB or lower by Standard & Poor's rating service or Ba or lower by Moody's rating service. Junk bonds carry a relatively high degree of risk but generally pay a high rate of return.

Keogh plan: A savings or investment plan for self-employed people whose purpose and benefits resemble those of the IRA. However, the Keogh plan allows a larger amount of money to be sheltered from income taxes each year. (*See also* individual retirement account.)

liquidity: The ease with which invested funds can be sold or otherwise converted to cash.

living trust: A trust which takes effect during the lifetime of the person who establishes it. At the death of the maker of the trust, probate is avoided and the assets can be immediately transferred to the beneficiary.

load: The commission charged by the firm that manages a mutual fund; normally a percentage of the amount invested.

margin: Cash or credit advanced by a broker to allow the purchase of stocks or bonds for only a fraction of the full price. Making such a purchase is known as *buying on margin.*

maturity: The date on which a loan must be paid, or the period during which the loan may remain outstanding.

money market: The market in which various kinds of high-yielding, short-term securities are bought and sold. Interest rates on the money market respond quickly to changes in financial and economic conditions.

money market deposit account: A bank account whose funds are invested in money market securities.

money market fund: A mutual fund which invests in money market securities.

mortgage: A loan made with the ownership of personal property, such as a house, given as collateral. If the loan is not repaid, the holder of the mortgage has a right to ownership of the property.

municipal bond: A bond issued by a state or local government or one of its agencies. Interest earned on municipal bonds is normally exempt from federal income tax, and sometimes from state and local income taxes as well.

mutual fund: An investment company that pools the funds of many individuals and invests them in stocks, bonds, or other securities. Those who invest through a mutual fund are called *shareholders* and receive dividends whose size depends on the performance of the fund's investments.

no-load fund: A mutual fund that does not charge a commission on investments.

option: A contract giving the right to buy or sell a specified quantity of stock at a specified price within a specified period of time.

par value: The value printed on the face of a stock or bond; often the same as the initial selling price. The resale price of a stock or bond usually differs from the par value.

pension: An arrangement in which regular payments are made to a retired employee by his or her former employer or by a government agency.

points: An interest charge levied by a mortgage lender at the time a house is sold. For each point charged, the buyer must pay the lending institution 1 percent of the mortgage amount. On some mortgages, no points are charged; on others, 3 points or more.

portfolio: The complete array of investment holdings belonging to an individual or an institution.

preferred stock: A security representing partial ownership in the issuing corporation. Holders of preferred stock have a prior claim to the earnings and assets of the company over holders of common stock. Preferred stock usually carries no stockholder voting privileges and usually pays a fixed annual dividend. (*See also* common stock.)

premium: (1) The amount of money paid to purchase a life insurance policy or an annuity. (2) The amount by which the selling price of stock or bond exceeds its face value or par value.

principal: An amount of money lent or invested.

probate: A process of carrying out the instructions of a will within the court system.

prospectus: A formal document prepared by a corporation issuing stocks, bonds, or other securities that is made available to all prospective buyers of the securities. The prospectus must include certain facts about the company and the security as specified by the Securities and Exchange Commission, including the names of the corporation's officers, as well as the corporation's financial condition and its recent record of profits and losses.

redemption: The repurchase of a bond or other form of indebtedness by the issuing corporation or government agency.

registered bond: A bond registered in its owner's name. Interest is paid at regular intervals to the registered owner; the bond may be transferred only by changing the registration.

reinvestment: (1) The practice of returning all or some of a company's profits to the business for use in financing growth, plant, or equipment purchases. (2) An arrangement whereby dividends or interest earned by shares in a mutual fund is automatically used to purchase additional shares in the fund.

return on investment: The amount of profit received on an investment as a percentage of the amount of capital invested. Also called *yield*.

reverse mortgage: A home loan that is treated in the opposite fashion of a standard mortgage because the money goes from the lender (bank) to the homeowner.

revocable living trust: A trust established during the grantor's lifetime in which a change or revocation can take place any time.

savings bank: A state-chartered financial institution which accepts deposits and offers loans at regulated interest rates.

savings and loan association: A financial institution, technically owned by depositors, which invests primarily in home mortgages.

Securities and Exchange Commission (SEC): The U.S. federal regulatory agency charged with controlling the issuing, buying, and selling of stocks, bonds, and other securities. The SEC supervises the operation of securities exchanges, registers brokers, and enforces laws governing the issuance of securities.

security: A written instrument that either certifies partial ownership of a business or promises repayment of a debt by a business or government agency.

shareholder: The owner of one or more shares of stock in a corporation or mutual fund.

simplified employee pension (SEP): A retirement plan for business owners, including those self-employed. An IRA is set up for each employee up to a maximum of $30,000 or 15 percent (13.043 percent if self-employed) of earnings.

stock: A share in the ownership of a corporation.

surrender value: The amount of money for which a life insurance policy may be redeemed prior to the death of the policyholder. In most cases, the surrender value of a policy increases annually during the life of the policy. Also called *cash value.*

tax bracket: The level at which an individual's income is taxed, normally determined by the size of his or her taxable income. The higher the taxable income, the higher the tax bracket and the higher the rate of taxation.

tax-deferred: Not subject to income tax until a later date.

tax-exempt: Not subject to income tax.

tax shelter: Any device or strategy by which a taxpayer can avoid paying income taxes on a portion of his or her income. Examples include individual retirement accounts (IRAs), Keogh plan accounts, 401(k) accounts, and certain limited partnerships.

term: The period of time during which an investment or an insurance policy is in effect.

term insurance: A form of life insurance in which the benefit is payable only if the insured person dies during a specified period.

testamentary trust: A trust which takes effect only after the death of the person who established it.

Treasury bill: A short-term obligation of the federal government, sold in minimum amounts of $10,000, with maturity periods of 3, 6, and 12 months. Treasury bills are sold at a discount from their face value; the discount represents prepayment of the interest on the loan. At maturity, the bill is redeemable for its full face value.

Treasury bond: A long-term obligation of the federal government, sold in minimum amounts of $1000, with maturity periods of 10 to 30 years. Treasury bonds are sold both by the federal government and in the secondary market, where the prices fluctuate in accordance with changes in interest rates.

Treasury note: An intermediate-term obligation of the federal government, sold in minimum amounts of $1000 or $5000 (depending upon maturity), with maturity periods of 1 to 10 years. Like Treasury bonds, Treasury notes are available on the secondary market at varying prices.

trust: An arrangement whereby property is transferred from one party, called the *trustor,* to a second party, called the *trustee,* for the benefit of a third party, called the *beneficiary.*

Trusts are usually established in order to reduce tax liability, streamline the transfer of assets after death, and/or maintain some control over the use of assets after they have been transferred.

unit trust: An investment plan in which an investor buys a share in a portfolio of corporate or municipal bonds. The investor receives a specified rate of interest on his or her investment payable over a specified period of time, depending on the maturity dates of the bonds in the portfolio.

universal life insurance: A type of life insurance policy in which part of the premium payment is used to provide life insurance protection and the remainder is invested in any of a variety of high-yielding instruments.

volume: (1)the number of shares of a particular stock that are bought or sold on a given day. (2) The total number of shares of stock that are bought or sold on an organized exchange on a given day.

whole life insurance: A type of life insurance policy in which premium payments are continued at the same level throughout the life of the policyholder, with death benefits payable whenever the policyholder dies.

will: A written document prepared according to legal specifications which provides for distribution of the writer's assets after his or her death.

yield: *See* return on investment.

zero coupon bond: A corporate, municipal, or Treasury bond sold at a discount from its face value. Upon maturity, the zero coupon bond is redeemed for the full face value, with the discount representing the interest earned on the investment.

About the Author

Joel Lerner has been a professor for over 30 years and is a former chairman of the Business Division at Sullivan County Community College, Loch Sheldrake, New York. He is the publisher of the *Middle/Fixed Income Letter*, a monthly personal financial newsletter, and has authored numerous textbooks that have sold more than a million copies. Mr. Lerner is a financial lecturer to several Fortune 500 firms, has produced his own TV and radio series, and addresses thousands of people every year on financial management. He lives in Monticello, New York.